CHILDREN: NOBLE CAUSES OR
WORTHY CITIZENS?

Children: Noble Causes or Worthy Citizens?

Karl Eric Knutsson

United Nations Children's Fund
INTERNATIONAL CHILD DEVELOPMENT CENTRE
Florence - Italy

Published by
Arena
Ashgate Publishing Limited
Gower House
Croft Road
Aldershot
Hants GU11 3HR
England

Ashgate Publishing Company
Old Post Road
Brookfield
Vermont 05036
USA

The contents of this book are the responsibility of the author and do not necessarily reflect the policies or views of the United Nations Children's Fund (UNICEF).

British Library Cataloguing in Publication Data

Knutsson, Karl Eric
  Children, noble causes or worthy citizens?
  1. Children – Social conditions   2. Children's rights
  I. Title
  305.2'3

ISBN 1 85742 420 4

Library of Congress Catalog Card Number:
Knutsson, Karl Eric
  Children: noble causes or worthy citizens? / Karl Eric Knutsson
      p.   cm.
  Includes bibliographical references and index.
  ISBN 1-85742-420-4 (hardback)
  1. Child welfare—Developing countries. 2. Child welfare—
  International cooperation. 3. Child development—Developing
  countries. 4. Child development—International cooperation.
  I. Title.
  HV804.K58   1997
  362.7'09172'4—DC21   97–19757
                                                                      CIP

Typeset in Palatino by Raven Typesetters, Chester
Printed in Great Britain at Biddles Ltd, Guildford and King's Lynn.

Contents

Foreword

This is a remarkable book, and I am happy to have been given this opportunity to introduce it through a brief foreword. In doing this I cannot avoid writing about the author. I wish to highlight his commitment and the visions which he extols both for a critical debate about development and for his dedication to and skills in translating them into meaningful and pragmatic international cooperation. The title of the introduction, 'Bridging Theory and Practice', aptly describes that to which he has devoted a great part of his talents and energies. This also explains the sympathy and the support with which so much of his work has been met especially in the countries of the South.

One has the impression that Karl Eric, taking long leaves from a promising academic career, was searching for ways to repay the gifts of knowledge and understanding that he had so generously been given by African peasants and nomads during his extensive experience in fieldwork. He was asked by the Swedish Parliament to design strategies to put knowledge to use for the battle against poverty and inequity in the world. The proposals which he inspired focused on utilizing, buttressing and building capacity for research especially in poor countries and on reorienting the Swedish and to some extent the international research community toward contributing meaningfully in these efforts. It is a pity that the results of the original contribution published in the book *Research for Development* did not appear in the major international languages. Released already in 1973, the book in many ways preceded and prepared the ground for other important works, such as the now classic *What Now?: Toward Another Development* backed by the Dag Hammarskjold Foundation.

Karl Eric became the founder and first director general of the Swedish Agency for Research Cooperation with Developing Countries (SAREC). It was in this context that we met in the mid-1970s. Although in research cooperation most of the initiatives were with African and some Asian countries, the support for research and for scientists and researchers in Latin America, especially during the difficult years of the 1970s, was critical. Contributing to building national capacity for research was one of SAREC's main priorities. But Karl Eric realized that in Latin America, where much capacity already existed, the main task was to preserve and protect that capacity from the onslaught of inhuman and oppressive regimes. Without going into the details, I would like to record the fact that in many circles of Latin America Karl Eric is still regarded as a worthy follower of Raoul Wallenberg in protecting the oppressed and the persecuted, among whom were a great number of researchers fighting for freedom of thought, for intellectual, political and ethical honesty and for human rights and democracy. Many were given an international shield and were even saved due to Karl Eric's flexible and unconventional use of the means of international scientific support. These were courageous and innovative activities. Three recipients of these 'protective' grants later became democratically elected presidents of their countries in Central and South America. In the region, these were years of great intellectual creativity which paved the way for a renewed understanding of the long-term economic, political and cultural foundations of security and human rights.

Following his distinguished academic and political career, Karl Eric chose to accept the invitation of one of the world's most honourable and respected leaders in international cooperation for human betterment, James P. Grant, and to join him at UNICEF as his deputy executive director, interspersing this service with work as the regional director of the UNICEF Eastern and Southern Africa Region and the UNICEF South Asia Region.

In the course of my activities as chairperson of the Preparatory Committee of the World Summit for Social Development which was held in Copenhagen in 1995, I consulted many people, among them Karl Eric Knutsson, whom I regard as an outstanding thinker and practitioner in planning for human betterment. He encouraged me greatly by supporting the idea that the conference was not only about social development; in his view, the initiative was an important step toward the security of humankind for the next century.

It is in the same spirit that he has written this book. It focuses on the 40 per cent of the global population who are children. As my notes about his career demonstrate, the book is written by a person who not only, as we all do, loves children, but who has also a thorough experience in science and social policy and many years of analysis and practical work in the field in all continents of the world.

In this book he is using his experience – with children and childhood as an entry point – to ask some fundamental questions about social and human development for the next century and how it can be achieved. He challenges us to reflect about the credibility of our theories and policies if we choose to neglect the presence of the nearly one-half of the global population who are children. He tries – and in this he makes a pioneering contribution – to over-come the sectoralization and the specialization in the development discourse and to combine historical, psychological, cultural, economic, political, human rights and development perspectives into a coherent whole. He courageously commutes among philosophical, theoretical, ethical and prag-matic issues and uses down-to-earth examples to illustrate complex prob-lems. In this way he tries to bring together debates which otherwise, and detrimentally for our understanding, are carried out in sectoral and disci-plinary isolation. He also proposes some simple first steps which can be taken immediately in moving towards making the Convention on the Rights of the Child a living instrument.

The author uses the perspective of the child to identify, analyse and discuss some of the major challenges for the future. In the process he provides us with a new basis for determining what so-called 'development' should be about and what changes are needed in economics, social studies and also to make the necessary political course corrections.

As an interested partner in the follow-up of the World Social Summit, I recommend this book as a piece worthy of serious study and reflection.

Juan Somavia
Permanent Representative to the United Nations of the Government of Chile and Chair of the Preparatory Committee of the World Summit for Social Development, and formerly of the Economic and Social Council (ECOSOC) and of the Security Council of the United Nations

Preface

At one point in this extraordinary book of essays on the international debate about betterment for children, Karl Eric Knutsson refers to a question we hear all too often in UNICEF circles: 'Who can be against children?'.

Professor Knutsson's analysis leads us very close to the conclusion that most of us border on being against children. We are surely against children – including future generations of children – when we poison our air and our rivers and demolish our forests, when we foment or tolerate racism, ethnic hatred, terrorism or societal violence, and when we spend obscene sums on weapons of personal or mass destruction at the expense of the simplest interventions needed to overcome hunger, malnutrition and fatal or disabling diseases attacking children. Less obviously, we are against children when we fail to treat them with respect, to recognize the importance for them of self-esteem and of their need to be loved and nurtured, but also when we fail to heed their need to be heard and to have their views taken into account as their families, communities and societies sort out a host of competing priorities for scarce resources and seek to achieve some sort of progress.

How can we claim, Karl Eric Knutsson goes on to ask, that our conceptual frameworks, our diagnostic tools, our policies for economic and social reform, and our ethical standards are valid in theory and useful in practice when they so often exclude the 40 per cent of the world's population which consists of the children and youth on this precarious planet?

In seeking to reframe the questions we ask (or fail to ask) ourselves, the author strikes out on a path on which few theoreticians or practitioners of development have dared to tread. He is wise enough and honest enough to bring a host of doubts and a healthy dose of humility to his search. He is seeking new approaches to betterment for children which are, first and foremost, ethically sound, but also conceptually powerful, as well as politically and programmatically viable. He goes far beyond his own announced intention to bridge theory and practice and to span the boundaries of academic disciplines and institutionalized sectors. The thoughtful reader – this is not a book for readers unwilling to think carefully and daringly – will find what may be the beginning of a genuinely original way for all of us concerned with children to conceptualize and visualize the main tasks which lie ahead: challenges lying far beyond the normal limits of our well-meaning but short-sighted plans and programmes for that neglected 40 per cent of our planet's population.

For those of us who have been concerned with making the rights of all children a reality, without discrimination of any kind, as recognized in the 1989 Convention on the Rights of the Child, these essays are a vivid reminder of several important facts.

First, organizations seriously concerned with the effective implementation of the Convention must be concerned as well with creating the underlying conditions necessary for the rights outlined in the Convention to become widely recognized and protected both by governments and by civil societies.

Second, the commitment of civil society, starting with families and small communities, is at least as important as that of governments, and the two levels of commitment are mutually reinforcing.

Third, the genuine participation and empowerment of children and youth are basic goals and, ultimately, essential tools for achieving the high principles which underlie the Convention, as well as the specific provisions contained in this historic international treaty.

Karl Eric Knutsson sums up his case for 'making a reality of the Convention' by urging that we avoid focusing narrowly on specific rights and instead 'envision betterment for children not only as the establishment of the rights of children, but also as the establishment of the duties of society'. The duties of society very much embrace the duties of parents and children. Children need to be given far more support and space in society to acquire the skills they need in order to survive and eventually gain productive employment, but also to acquire the social and cultural skills, as well as the sound ethical values, including respect for the rights and dignity of others, on which betterment for both children and society must ultimately rest. Far too often adults deny children this vital space which they need to develop the skills and values necessary to mature and meet their responsibilities. In so doing, unwittingly or deliberately, adults are acting against the best interests of children and damaging the prospects for the betterment of all society.

In my view, it is a hopeful sign that UNICEF has seen fit to enable Karl Eric Knutsson to write these essays. The careful reader, conscious of the implications of the author's measured prose, will detect elements of self-criticism of UNICEF's tendency to zero in with such determination on children, especially infants and young children, that we sometimes neglect or ignore the complex and rapidly changing economic, technological, social and political setting and the historical context in which organized efforts to save and protect vulnerable children must operate. If we are to move children towards the centre of politics and policymaking, as the author seeks to encourage us to do with his writings, a well-grounded understanding of the larger forces at work in society is essential for all who share a commitment to that goal.

These essays are written especially for 'reflective practitioners' and 'far-sighted politicians' (if any remain), but also for the more contemplative scholars who seek to develop conceptual frameworks, paraphrasing Gunnar Myrdal, which can actually hold reality. I can speak for all of my colleagues at the UNICEF International Child Development Centre, who have benefited immensely from Karl Eric Knutsson's work with us as a senior fellow, in urging each of these audiences to read with care, reflect with bold vision and join us in this challenging process of creating the conditions for the emergence of the citizen child.

James R. Himes
UNICEF International Child Development Centre

Acknowledgements

Thanks to a few will have to stand in for gratitude to many.

I am indebted to the late James P. Grant, with whom I have had the privilege of working over the last 15 years, both in the field and in the room next door, for inspiring and challenging leadership and for offering me a period of reflection and study as senior research fellow at the International Child Development Centre in the Spedale degli Innocenti in Florence.

I also wish to thank James R. Himes of the International Child Development Centre for his frequent advice and his extensive, detailed comments during various phases of the work.

Thomas Matthai has constantly stressed the need to trust the people. I have cherished his thoughtful advice during my recent years in South Asia, and his ideas have continued to be active participants in my work. He has also carefully scrutinized an early draft of these essays.

Giovanni Andrea Cornia and Carlos Castillo, programme directors at the Florence Centre, have questioned and encouraged me through the process of searching and searching again that we call research.

Richard Jolly has combined a heavy management burden with enquiries into basic issues of human-centred betterment. I am especially appreciative of his thoughtful reflections on a new development approach for children.

Mary Racelis, George Kent, Mike Edwards, Urban Jonsson, Paolo Viazzo, Mark Kelly and others have generously and conscientiously reviewed and commented on various versions of the emerging text and have done their best to make it meaningful and readable and to rein in my sometimes encyclopedic ambitions. Any failure in these regards is in spite of their sacrifices.

I have benefited greatly from the editorial guidance of Robert Zimmermann, who has worked hard to improve clarity and weed out clumsy formulations.

I also thank Mickey Cibardo, who has helped to put the first drafts together and who has literally waded through meandering ideas and streams of hand-scribbled notes.

Last and most, Pauline O'Dea has supported me with patience, compassion, constructive criticism and advice.

Karl Eric Knutsson

Introduction: Bridging theory and practice

'All ethics so far evolved rest upon a single premise: that the individual is a member of a community of interdependent parts.'[1]

'There is no touchstone, except the treatment of childhood, which reveals the true character of a social philosophy more clearly than the spirit in which it regards the misfortunes of those of its members who fall by the way.'[2]

This book is about children and development, as distinct from the development of children. It deals mainly with the nature and location of the public and especially the international debate on children. The discussion is part of ongoing efforts aimed at changing the discourse on children and strengthening the theoretical, ethical and political arguments for taking children seriously.[3]

The many contexts of the debate

Development for children is a complex subject, full of seeming contradictions. During recent decades there has been significant progress in improving the lives of children in many areas. In 1990 the goal of universal child immunization was declared to have been reached. Although gaps have appeared in this protective coverage in some countries since then, the situation is still generally better than ever before. Now, each year more than 100 million infants receive four or five immunizations before their first birthdays, and it has been estimated that three million children are being saved annually as a result.[4]

The prevalence of malnutrition is exhibiting a downward trend almost everywhere except in Africa. Between 1975 and 1990 the proportion of underweight children in Asia and Latin America fell from 42 to 34 per cent. In

1

Thailand alone the share of underweight children declined from 36 to 13 per cent between 1982 and 1990.[5] Significant progress is also being made in the critical area of micronutrient deficiencies.

Although 1.2 billion people are still denied access to safe drinking water, slightly more than this number – around 1.3 billion people – achieved improved access during the 1980s. The number of those within a reasonable distance of a water source has increased from 10 to 60 per cent in the rural developing world. However, the use of environmental sanitation facilities is much lower.[6]

Primary education enrolments, which have a significant influence on social indicators such as mortality and fertility rates, have gone up everywhere, particularly among girls. Between 1960 and 1990 enrolments rose from just under one-half to almost three-quarters of primary school age children. Nonetheless, because of population growth, more children in South Asia, for example, are out of school than ever before. Almost 130 million children around the world do not have access to primary education, and only one-third of the girls born today will complete primary education. About one billion people, many of them women, will be illiterate at the end of the century.

As demonstrated by indicators such as infant mortality and life expectancy, some threats to health and life are being reduced. However, poverty still afflicts the lives of vast numbers of people in many developing countries. The expansion of markets dominated by private interests and the global drive towards economic and fiscal restructuring are generally biased against the weakest members of society and thereby diminish the capacity of these people to improve their life chances.[7] Conventional development theories of whatever stripe have not been able to anticipate, clarify or otherwise solve the problems generated by the resurgence of poverty and by mounting ethnic conflicts and other social disruptions in many parts of the world.[8] Unemployment, discrimination, homelessness, the exploitation and abuse of children, violence, the alienation of youth and drug trafficking have escalated dramatically. The fabric of social life is undergoing significant and rapid transformations, but the direction in which these changes are taking us and the resulting social consequences are far from obvious. Communities face the daunting task of recognizing, understanding and dealing with problems which are constantly being defined and redefined.

Since the International Year of the Child in 1979, advocacy for children has intensified. The Convention on the Rights of the Child has propelled these concerns and efforts decisively into the political debate over human rights. The follow-up to the World Summit for Children – the national plans of action, the endeavour to foster improvements in budgetary allocations and official development assistance for children, and the call for 'children first' – is illustrative of the attempts to translate the ethical energy which has been stirred into political action.

Attempts to construct and support the theoretical and empirical under-pinnings for a fresh approach to children and childhood are also intensifying. Most developing countries are now producing regular reports on the situation of children within their borders. The European project, 'Childhood as a Social Phenomenon', has involved an ambitious and comparative regional analysis. Academic attention is becoming more focused on issues linked with childhood, and the number of commentaries on various aspects of the Convention on the Rights of the Child is growing.

However, all this has still had little effect on the dominant discourses in social science, economics and politics. Thus, although we seem to be witnessing a reinforcement of advocacy and of programmes for the betterment of children, both the debate on children and the policies aimed at them continue to suffer from pervasive theoretical weaknesses and from a dearth of relevant data. This is persistently constraining political articulation and action. More serious and effective consideration of the interfaces among ethical concern, theoretical understanding and political energy is required, and ways to improve the design and joint implementation of advocacy, knowledge and political initiative must be found.

Despite recent positive changes children remain largely marginalized, especially politically. In the majority of poor countries, they are for the most part invisible, penetrating the public conscience when disasters, generally caused by adults, convert their suffering into headlines and media footage. In better-off countries, children are frequently without meaningful contacts with the workplace and the other environments of adults. Many spend a major part of their time in schools, daycare centres and other institutions dedicated to children, or with their peers. Like the elderly, they are often regarded as a nuisance by people of productive age. Such careless attitudes are sometimes masked by the abundance of the material goods, favoured by producers and consumers alike, to compensate for the social and emotional neglect.

Thus, in comparison to other theoretically and politically acknowledged categories and structures of society, childhood tends to be unrecognized, misrepresented and misunderstood, although every society clearly identifies a defined period of time in the individual's life as childhood. The dominant perception, which is increasingly becoming a standard notion of childhood throughout the world, is an extension of a romanticized Western view which regards children as essentially isolated from the rest of society.

Childhood constitutes a key cultural and social category within all societies. It is the accepted and legitimate framework within which children are located and organized and through which they migrate on their way towards a wider society. Childhood is firmly embedded in society and children are important members of, and actors in, society. Children therefore need to be understood in their own right and not merely as targets of social action. This calls for vigorous advocacy against the notion of the isolated child and the child as property, whether of adult society or of the state.

These are significant issues which, although they are not new, must be patiently thought through if we wish to raise the visibility of children and stimulate action for the betterment of their situation and their future. We need to ask questions about our perceptions of children and childhood, about the ways these perceptions emerge to influence and shape our assumptions, preferences and choices concerning them and about the manner in which these assumptions, preferences and choices, in turn, condition the ability of children to affect our perceptions.

There are signs that the public, and sometimes official, rhetoric is changing towards 'children first' and child rights. However, this does not mean that there is a universal consensus that children are important. Children (like other minorities) and the problems of children are often overlooked. They are among the chief victims of war and poverty; millions of them are exploited and abused as cheap labour or as commodities in national and international sex markets.

Indeed, the steps which have been taken towards a greater recognition of the rights of the child have been small, especially in comparison with the many needs of children, the obligations which adult society places on children and the contributions which children actually make. Although the nature of and the relationships between children's rights and their obligations differ significantly among the various phases of childhood and also in relation to adults, it is usually forgotten that children are brought into life mainly within the context of important and demanding obligations. They are expected to provide emotional and social gratification and later also often support and assistance to parents and other caregivers. This represents an obligation – rather than a right – placed on children from the beginning. Other obligations are associated with the social and cultural reproduction of society. These require that children perform duties defined by adults related to learning, education and schooling. Adult society also defines the obligations and sets the rules for children in managing their overall physical, biological, mental and social growth.

The issue of children's rights must be put in the proper context of these massive obligations placed on children and collectively on childhood. The argument is not that children should be freed from obligations but that, if these obligations are not recognized and understood, the work to promote the rights of children will suffer correspondingly.

Many other factors contribute to condition the nature, the biases and the surprising limitations of our knowledge about children and childhood. One is a lack of the fundamental child-specific data and information – especially from the perspective of the child – which is required for a better theoretical understanding of children's situations and for policy and advocacy purposes.

Another factor which has had significant consequences for the nature and the location of the debate on children stems from the specific tradition in which the concept of child development has been used. Until recently 'child development' covered mainly the physical, psychological and to some extent the social growth of the individual child.

The development of children – as distinct from development or betterment for children – has been defined as the process of the increasing 'rationality' of children, in their play and other activities, as they evolve through a sequence of maturing steps to the ultimate goal of adulthood. In this process children are perceived as beings queuing to acquire the cognitive and rational skills which will allow them to leave 'primitive' childhood behind them. This view of the development of children needs to be changed along the lines suggested by researchers who demand recognition and respect, theoretically and ethically, for children and childhood in their own right and on their own terms.

The sectoralization and specialization of social studies, including enquiries into the nature and problems of childhood, are affecting and sometimes distorting our understanding of the situations and problems of children. Efforts to bridge the widening chasm between human experience and scientific abstraction must be encouraged. This must involve a rethinking of theoretical assumptions and of the prevalent approaches of social, economic and cultural studies.

Children are also being neglected by 'developmentalism', which, since it was first articulated in the eighteenth century, has become the credo behind the faith in economic and social progress. As many have pointed out, the ideology of developmentalism has been dominated by neoclassical economics. Economics must certainly remain a key dimension – although not the primary one – in any theory of human betterment. However, to serve this important purpose, economics as a discipline and as a profession must change. For this to occur, economics must be deepened and broadened so that it takes in all relevant dimensions of 'reality', which after all is broader and deeper in terms of convictions, beliefs, meaning and values than the material resources, technology and economic transactions governing the world view of the 'market'. The assumed ability of the individual to make 'rational' choices has become idolized as the essential characteristic of economic and social actors. This concept of Man needs to be complemented by a concept of the social actor who exists in relation to others and who therefore needs to plan and to undertake activities with others in mind.

There are many reasons for the exclusion of children and other marginalized groups in the economic and developmental calculus. The capitalist and the socialist approaches to development are based on a positivist tradition in natural science. Development theorists have abstracted from reality what they judge essential for their explanatory purposes and have left out factors which they feel do not fit. Children, women, minorities and even average people in ordinary communities either do not matter in this calculus or do not fit within the dominant models. Consequently, they have been neglected.

The world is witnessing a phenomenon of accelerating technological, economic and cultural 'globalization'. Children and childhood are rarely discussed within these larger contexts. However, if we want to include children in our debate on development and betterment, we must understand their situation from this perspective as well. This requires that we redefine the space-time dimension in policies and planning to include international and intergenerational concerns.

Serious attention must also be paid to the child's lack of power. In a time of expanding democracy, the importance of voters is increasing, and there is a parallel inflation in the attention which politicians give to potential blocks of voters. Since the legal voting age is usually associated with the generally accepted age when adolescents reach maturity, children do not constitute an attractive pool of voters who must be courted. In the competition for resources, they thus often lose out to other groups. This imbalance is increasingly affecting the allocation of resources for child-related causes.

Finding ways to recognize, and respond to, a child population which for many valid reasons cannot articulate or defend its own basic interests is a crucial challenge for the democratic system of governance.

Bridging theory and practice

It is tempting to reflect and write about children at close distance and in the near perspective. Being with children sweeps away theoretical considerations of time and space. In the often quoted words of the Chilean poet Gabriella Mistral, 'the name of the child is today'. The laughter of a child turns fragmented attention into an intensive experience of the present. The needs of a suffering child are immediate and urgent. Time is now and space is here. The quality and intensity in our relationship with children tend to be transformed into anæmic abstractions when we try to examine them in the broader perspectives of the adult world of planning, governance and the rhetoric of development. Nonetheless, we need to remember that both the close perspective and the more long-term and sometimes theoretical perspective are necessary. If children are to become truly incorporated into our public and professional responsibilities, we must consider them in different contexts and on several levels. We must analyse perceptions, articulate language and create conceptual frameworks which can deepen our understanding and help us in practical work.

The literature on development and on various facets of the situation of children is extensive, although it has not been sufficiently linked. It is understandable if many people feel that what can be said has already been said. However, in order to be able to reflect meaningfully, we must dare to dissect prevailing conventions and official rhetoric. Only then can we hope to achieve a better understanding of dominant perceptions and the assumptions behind them, and suggest ways to foster the needed change.

From wherever we may come and whatever avenue we may choose to follow, we must begin with an idea of what ought to constitute the good society in which adults would want to cherish children and in which children would want to live and grow, a society which does not require special programmes for children, women, minorities or any other neglected groups because it has been built on respect, decency, equity and the effective joint management of the needs of all. If such a society could be established, it would be likely to find solutions for most problems, including those experienced by children. However, it does not take much reflection to realize that this goal is far from being achieved; it may even be completely utopian. Indeed, there are signs that the good society, or at least a more tolerable and decent one for all people, including children, is becoming more and more difficult to attain. Whatever the case may be, we cannot continue to wait for the good society to occur. We must therefore continue, while working to establish a better society, to pay special attention to children through well-considered initiatives.

The discussion in these essays revolves around the nature and the location of the debate on children and childhood within the larger debate on development. Because of increasing administrative and professional specialization, the debate on children and betterment for children has been disjointed into separate and often isolated sociological, psychological, cultural, historical, political and economic aspects. Likewise, the understanding of the problems and needs of children has been fragmented by often highly sectorized discussions in the fields of health, education, nutrition, sanitation, etc. We must break down the walls of these carefully constructed compartments and build bridges not only between theory and practice, but also between various disciplines and different fields of practice. This demands that we try to discuss children and childhood within all the relevant dimensions which surround them and affect them and which in turn are influenced by them.

The essay provides a helpful format for this endeavour. The word 'essay' signifies 'attempt' or 'the action or process of trying'.[9] It is used to refer to short, discursive and rather general pieces which summarize an often personal explanation of evidence and which are aimed at provoking further reflection. It is not intended to be a wholly rigorous, well-documented piece of work. Furthermore, the essay is meant to be employed to explore possibilities and suggest interpretations rather than to cover a subject systematically. The format is especially appropriate for an informal examination of issues and for asking questions about the nature of the questions one is asking. Moreover, essays in a collection can usually be somewhat more independent of each other than can chapters in a book. This fosters greater freedom for exploration than might be available if stricter criteria of logical flow and structural consistency were applied. It also allows wider variation in the approaches to diverse issues.

These essays are intended to contribute to the efforts to move children towards the centre of politics and policymaking and to indicate some possible ways in which this can be achieved. This is one of the major challenges of our time.

In order to offer a reasonable basis for this discussion, we must touch on many areas, including perceptions of children, the available knowledge on childhood, the absence of the subject of children in political and economic discourse and the many other invisibilities of children. We must also try to understand the effects on children of the massive transformations which societies have undergone because of industrialization, urbanization, the expansion of the market economy, accelerating globalization in many fields, and the accompanying 'atomization' in the structure of social relationships in most countries.

Although the theoretical basis for such an exploration ought to be as sturdy as possible, the purpose should also be practical. The guiding principle should be the need to identify several first steps which are necessary, sensible and possible to take. Furthermore, if we want to translate the Convention on the Rights of the Child into reality, as we must do, we have to seek beyond the professional constituencies, non-government organizations and other agencies which are concerned with the betterment of children. We must also convince a great number of other professional constituencies, as well as academics, politicians, policymakers and planners. We must create a genuine sense of involvement throughout society.

In attempting this, we should seriously consider ways to link children's issues to the environmental movement. We must begin to realize that we forget children when we cut down forests. We forget children when we poison our rivers and our air. We forget children when we allow billions to be spent on weapons of mindless destruction and virtually nothing on the simple things which protect and sustain young lives. We forget children when we tolerate violence, racism, terrorism, economic enslavement, social injustice and political callousness, all of which deny to the millions their equal share in the common heritage of this planet. We forget children when we hate each other, when we kill each other and when we damage the world which we are holding in trust for children. If we cannot do for children the same as we do for seals and try to do for trees and rivers, then there is little hope for these other ambitions.

Likewise, we cannot hope to improve the conditions in which children live if we forget gender equity and justice. Through the profound experiences of pregnancy, birth and nursing and through the key role of women in the family, the early phases of children's lives are interwoven with the lives of women. Because of this special relationship and despite all the many facets of this relationship, children frequently represent a major obstacle in many countries, if not most, for the struggle of women against gender inequities and for more independence. Thus there is often a complex, ambiguous, but also analogous relationship between the 'best interests' of women and the 'best interests' of the child. As Frances Olsen has pointed out:

> The neglect and abuse of children are often part and parcel of the neglect and abuse of women. As the predominant caretakers of children, women are greatly influenced by the role and status of children. Where conditions are good for children, they are generally good for women. Where society neglects and abuses children, it is likely to neglect and abuse women.[10]

There can be no doubt that the role of women as the primary caregivers for children has contributed to the impoverishment and dependency of women and that sometimes the 'legal protection of children can be and has been used as a basis for controlling women'.[11] Only by considering the two perspectives and the two constellations of potential and actual 'best interests' can we hope to minimize the risk that the betterment of one situation will result in the deterioration of the other.

We must also support the aspirations, though still weak, among men to share in the responsibility for children. Following the biological pregnancy and physical birth, there is among the human species a prolonged period of 'social' pregnancy, leading, as it were, to many subsequent births of the child into different phases of childhood and widening circles of society.[12] These 'pregnancies' and these 'births' can and must become a shared responsibility involving men together with women and increasingly children themselves.[13]

Each of these challenges relating to the environment, the role of women, gender equity and the involvement of men in childraising would merit a separate essay. The same is true for the many specific situations which can only be touched on as illustrations rather than through careful analysis, including children in war, child labour, the sexual exploitation of children and the children among the enormous numbers of refugees, ethnic minorities, unwanted immigrants and the homeless on the streets of the expanding cities.

The nature of the debate about children and development – or the absence of such a debate – will determine our awareness and our perceptions and thereby shape our responses and proposals for action. A discussion of the form and location of the debate itself is, therefore, a necessary prerequisite to a more programme-related approach.[14] To enhance the usefulness of the contribution, the emphasis in the essays is on aspects of the debate which have been neglected or which have not yet received sufficient attention, as well as on controversial issues of which practitioners and advocates need to be aware in order to formulate credible arguments and meaningful strategies.

In rushing to do what we believe is necessary and good we rarely give much thought to the nature of the fundamental assumptions and values which inform and guide our work. Why were certain crucial choices made concerning goals and strategies? Why were they made at a certain moment? What were the contexts in which these decisions were taken? What were the theoretical and practical justifications? Were such choices made because of some general ambition to be 'kind' to children, or were they mainly translations of some general trends within the larger development 'industry' rather than the result of theoretically and ethically trustworthy insights?

Instead of pausing to ask such questions, we tend to concentrate on day-to-day pressures, on technicalities and on organizational and other challenges. This leaves us ill equipped when we need to evaluate and explain what we are doing. It tempts us to dismiss important questions from supporters and critics alike with the emotional but rarely convincing counter question, 'Who can be against children?'. In doing so we not only weaken our own case but also the case for children.

In order to avoid such negative, albeit unintended, consequences we have to recognize and understand more clearly the linkages between the situation of children – and thereby of our work with them – and the major processes of development, including changes in economies and lifestyles and the overall social, cultural and political environments in which children live. We must recognize and correct a widespread misunderstanding according to which practical and ethical relevance is believed to diminish the theoretical quality of our enquiries. This seems to be a rather recent piece of mythology emerging from isolated academic communities which are searching to justify their very isolation and to establish internal systems of rules and rewards.

Many within the community of 'practitioners' suffer from similar prejudices. The special technical expertise and methodological competence provided by the knowledge community are valued and are in demand, but more exploratory and philosophical questions tend to be dismissed as unpractical. This can be a very unpractical mistake. To devote part of our analytical energy to some of the fundamental factors which may condition our mindsets, influence what we see and colour the glasses we all carry, knowingly or not, is therefore a very practical proposition. Indeed, we need not fear asking fundamental questions about what we are doing and about the nature of the perceptions and assumptions on which our strategies and our actions are built. What we must fear is not doing so, for, in the final analysis, that is a sure recipe for ending up – in the words of Bertrand Russell – being brilliantly wrong.

In his book on the principles of social solidarity, Hechter points to the urgent need to identify and respect the linkages between individual and collective action and between theoretical assumptions and what we believe to be empirical facts or 'practical knowledge'. He warns convincingly of the dangers of unreflected practice.

> Though evidence is necessary to test the limit of any theory, radical empiricism is unlikely to provide sociology's salvation. In the first place, most research is covertly theoretical. Because all descriptions are partial, investigators tend to rely on implicit theories to guide their collection of facts. This procedure introduces unknown (and often unknowable) assumptions, setting the stage for Alfred Marshall's admonishment that the most reckless and treacherous of all theorists is the one who professes to let the facts and figures speak for themselves.... Without explicit theories, there is no way to decide on [the] relative importance of facts. A democracy of facts too often degenerates into anarchy.[15]

In the background one can hear the warning of John Maynard Keynes that 'practical men in authority who believe themselves to be quite exempt from any intellectual influences are usually the slaves of some defunct economist.'[16] For our purposes, perhaps we should read 'some defunct assumptions'.

The discussion of these issues is not an attempt to respond merely to an academic desire to research and debate. It represents an effort to establish a dialogue with the many practitioners from a variety of national, cultural and professional settings who are concerned that a lack of time for reflection is negatively affecting the strength of their arguments, the credibility of their advocacy and the quality of their work.[17]

This points to the urgency of understanding the interface between theory and practice. Such an undertaking would require fundamental changes in the approaches usually adopted in the production of knowledge and the 'management' of practice.[18] This represents an enormous agenda, and here we can only underline the importance of these concerns and try to be sufficiently mindful of the nature of actual situations so that our discussions do not become divorced from reality.

The ambition to participate in a critical debate without losing touch with practical realities and common sense creates several challenges. One is related to the style of the discussion which often calls forth quite complicated philosophical reflections. To give context and meaning to these reflections, the essays contain stories about children. The stories are told simply, but, like life itself, they raise complex questions about the nature and purpose of knowledge and about our responsibility to seek, understand and manage knowledge for the betterment of children.

Another major challenge stems from a complication in language. The concept of development is a very perplexing one. Already in the 1960s Dudley Seers pointed out that the terminology had been so abused that it had lost most of its meaning.[19] Several decades later we face the same dilemma that

Seers faced. The language of development is very much alive and has in many ways become a global idiom. When a technical concept and the underlying ideologies which the concept represents have become as pervasive as have the concept and ideologies of development, it is very difficult to avoid them if we wish to communicate. The only way out is to try to clear the fog around the term and to apply the term critically and, if possible, restrictively. Nonetheless, we also need to propose an alternative and more precise language which might serve to capture the nature of the purposes and strategies of development more accurately than does the very broad and often ambiguous term 'development'.

The word 'betterment' fulfils some of these criteria. In contrast to the word 'development', it clearly indicates purpose and direction. It is not tainted by the ideological assumptions and the technocratic biases of the concept 'development'. Although references to 'development' cannot be avoided, the terminology of human betterment should be used whenever feasible.

The discussion which follows is divided into two parts. Part I identifies and examines major features of the debate on betterment for children. It deals with the many environments of the child, including the environments of poverty and culture and the space of childhood. It contains a story about one child and her encounters with the many environments which in one form or another affect all children; it identifies in practical terms and from the perspective of this child many of the issues with which the essays deal. This story is woven into a discussion of the cultural and social variations in the perceptions concerning children and is followed by an overview of the history of childhood and the beginnings of public concern for children.

These excursions serve as stepping stones for an examination of the nature and location of the debate on children, childhood and the betterment of the situation of children. This involves a look at some of the major perspectives, interests and other factors – theoretical, political and ethical – which are influencing and conditioning the debate. It also involves an inspection of the ways the debate has been translated into practice through various efforts at international cooperation for the betterment of children.

In Part II, several conclusions are drawn from the analysis of the debate. One essay deals with some of the assumptions, conceptual frameworks and methodological approaches within social and humanistic studies. It makes suggestions on steps to improve these and thereby enhance our ability to identify and analyse child-related problems. It argues that there is a need to move away from the inherited or conventional perceptions towards more solidly based insights, as well as a need to combine a more holistic 'thinking' about children with a pragmatic selectivity in initiatives and development programmes.

Another essay discusses major aspects of the ideology and theory of development. The focus is on the absence of children especially in macroeconomic analyses and policies.

The final essay proposes political and practical lessons which may be learned from the review of the nature and the location of the debate about children. Starting from a discussion of the Convention on the Rights of the Child, it suggests priorities in the creation of a social and political environment conducive to the translation of children's rights from ethical concerns to practical reality.

The neglect of children has two causes: lack of understanding and lack of interest. These essays aim to deepen both understanding and interest by clarifying the theoretical, ethical and pragmatic reasons for transforming the political neglect of children, as well as the other forms of neglect, into recognition and action. The essays raise questions rather than provide answers in order to stimulate thinking which will favour better practices. They are not about UNICEF, which has facilitated the work, but primarily about children, whose importance surpasses any specific institutional perspective.

Every author has an audience in mind. I dedicate these essays to the searching general reader, to reflective practitioners, including my friends and colleagues in UNICEF, to concerned students of human betterment and to the far-sighted politicians who are open to a demanding theoretical reflection and at the same time are committed to promoting the well-being of children through considered and compassionate action.[20]

Finally, these essays aim to build bridges between theory and practice. They emphasize serving rather than merely observing, acting rather than merely reacting, the need to reach the unreached and listen to the unheard and the need to stimulate the formation of new partnerships for joint popular, political and professional cooperation in a movement for, with and around children.

Notes and references

1. Aldo (1982), page 2.
2. Tawney (1926), page 239.
3. The phrase 'theoretical, ethical and political arguments' is used here in a commonsensical and approximative way. It raises many problems which cannot possibly be handled within the scope of this book. Science and ethics both consist of theory and practice. These are dialectically related in the sense that theory has no meaning without practice and practice has no meaning without theory. However, the two terms are used in this text in a somewhat 'looser' way, whereby 'theoretical' refers to well-considered arguments and their foundations; 'ethical' covers issues which may also be called 'moral', and 'practical' refers to actions and activities and their management. I am thankful to Urban Jonsson for his advice on these complexities.
4. UNICEF (1994), page 5.

5.   UNICEF (1994), page 5.
6.   UNICEF (1994), page 5.
7.   A debate on these issues was initiated by UNICEF in the mid-1980s and has led to a continuing international discussion on adjustment measures and social polity. See, for example, Cornia, Jolly and Stewart (1987).
8.   See, for example, Glazer and Moynihan (1975), Horowitz (1985), Gurr (1993), Stavenhagen (1990) and Moynihan (1993).
9.   OUP (1971), page 896.
10. Olsen (1992). See also Oakley (1993) and Alanen (1994).
11. Olsen (1992), page 193.
12. For a detailed discussion of the biological and social specificity of pregnancy and the early phases of childhood in humans, see Morgan (1994).
13. For example, see Richardson (1995). See also Levine (1994) and Bruce *et al* (1995).
14. Robert Myers has discussed major theoretical and programmatic issues in early child development programmes. Many of his observations and proposals have relevance for the broader issues of child-related development and human development in general. See Myers (1992).
15. Hechter (1987), page 2.
16. John Maynard Keynes here quoted from Corbridge (1994).
17. This particular formulation of a common view is based on a statement by Farid Rahman at the UNICEF meeting 'Strategies for Children', Bangkok, 1992.
18. The following are among those who have been especially instrumental in bringing these issues to the fore in social theory and in the debate on human betterment: Bourdieu (1977) and (1990), Ortner (1984), Uphoff (1992), Maxwell (1984) and Chambers (1993). See also Knutsson (1986).
19. Seers (1969), cited in Baster (1972), page 24.
20. For the mention of 'reflective practitioners', I am indebted to Edwards (1995). See also the discussion of research and practice in Edwards (1994).

Part I

The nature and location of the debate

Most debates about children deal with the characteristics of the various age groups, their skills and talents, or their concrete needs and problems. However, the discussion here will focus on the following questions:

- How has our understanding been conditioned by our knowledge of the many environments of the child, including the physical environment, the social and cultural environment, and the environment of poverty?
- How do perceptions change over time? Are they different in different cultures? What role do our perceptions of children and childhood play in shaping our knowledge and guiding our understanding?
- How do our interests in children, the purposes of our knowledge about them and the different vantage points from which we look at them colour our perceptions?
- How has the broader public concern for children been translated into policies and actions? What can we learn about changing perspectives on children and childhood from the choices made over the years by UNICEF, the international 'lead' agency for children?

Essay 1: The many environments of the child

If we wish to understand the situation of a substantial number of children today, we need to look at childhood in all relevant contexts including the large ones. We need to identify processes affecting children on all levels and in the major dimensions of the technological, political, economic and informational reality which influence the conditions of childhood.

To build an adequate knowledge base, to identify problems more precisely and to design relevant child-centred strategies, we must follow a holistic path to understanding. Only then can we hope to ask meaningful questions, learn helpful lessons regarding the planned and unplanned transformations which affect children and their childhood and design meaningful cooperative initiatives to assess and address problems.

Changing contexts of children and childhood

Social reality is a constantly changing arena in which internal and external processes combine to create the opportunities and raise the barriers which influence the physical, mental and spiritual well-being of the members of society, including children. The ultimate outcomes of these processes, especially on children, need to be carefully mapped.

The major processes which generate change are controlled and guided by those who have access to sufficient power and resources, whether globally or locally. The powerless, not least children, are especially susceptible to the negative effects of these processes. Effective monitoring and evaluation are required to recognize the effects of these processes and to erect and strengthen the defences against any unacceptable aberrations to which these processes might lead. Planned development initiatives must be constantly monitored in order to gauge their impact, whether positive or negative, on children. The advocacy over the last decade against economic adjustment

17

measures which are insensitive to social costs provides an illustration of how such monitoring might be accomplished. However, this sort of advocacy must be widened to include other major global economic and political phenomena such as the expansion of the market economy and the accompanying culture of consumerism and social fragmentation.

If we wish to learn from the changes surrounding the child, we have several choices. We can choose to look at the child's immediate environment, neighbourhood or community; we can choose to examine the social category and class into which the child has been born, and we can choose to analyse the nation in which the child grows. However, we must also understand what is happening in the world at large.

The child is usually associated with the smaller circles of family, home and neighbourhood. Yet, these are increasingly being moulded by outside processes. Children are living and acting locally, but are being influenced or manipulated more and more by global forces. The child is embedded in her or his environment and is affected by every aspect of human life. Therefore, an understanding of her life, the environment in which she lives and the problems which she faces can be reached only through reliance on many disciplines and theoretical traditions. To establish communication among these is essential if we wish to gain a holistic view which reflects reality. However, it is probably not possible to create an appropriate interdisciplinary language. We must therefore document – and hopefully agree on – the nature of the territory in which the child lives. We must also improve communication by exploring each set of conditions from the many angles of our various specialties. When we attempt to examine specific aspects or problems in children's lives, we must keep in mind the important features of the total environment of the child and the many phases through which she migrates within the temporal space of her childhood.

An environment of many poverties

The inevitable starting point is the situation of the child in a landscape of poverty. This is not a new story; it has been told repeatedly. Nonetheless, it needs to be revisited in order to keep it in the foreground of the debate on betterment for children.

Poverty and poverty-generating processes are key factors in determining the quality of life of large numbers of people, including children, throughout the world. Despite indicators suggesting that there are some positive trends (for example, in life expectancy and literacy), the proportion of the poor, however poor may be defined, appears to be stubborn in large parts of Africa, Asia and Latin America and to be growing rapidly in many countries even in the developed world.

Nor is there just the one poverty consisting of a lack of financial resources. There are many poverties constraining the lives of the poor and limiting their opportunities on all levels: the poverty of knowledge (despite the impressive amounts of very relevant knowledge accumulated over generations), the poverty of health, the poverty of power over one's own life, the poverty of social relationships and the poverty of deficient habitats and damaged environments. In turn, these poverties contribute to the poverty of confidence and the poverty of self-respect and dignity. Indeed, much of our understanding is distorted because of our fixation on the economic aspects of poverty.

The poor

Who then are the poor? We can roughly estimate their number. Some 800 million people in the world live in or near conditions of material poverty.[1] Among these, children are the largest group. Together with women, they form nearly three-fourths of the poor.

The income of a poor family may be so low that bare minimum consumption requirements cannot be met. Lacking productive assets and marketable skills, such a family cannot contribute fully to the development process or receive much gain from it. It is likely that the family is in debt to a local money lender. None of the family members are employed in the organized formal sector of the economy, although some of the members may be engaged in self-employment or wage-employment of an irregular nature and at low wage rates. Even young children may be involved in economic activity in order to supplement the family income.

The family is likely to live in a chronically poverty-stricken zone, in hilly or otherwise difficult terrain, in an area frequently subject to drought or flood, or in a slum in the very heart of a city. The family usually belongs to an economically backward or socially depressed class, occupational category, caste or tribe. It is unlikely to benefit from many public utilities or subsidized services like electricity, transportation, communications or institutional credit. Chances are that the family lives in a dingy one-room hut and lacks access to safe drinking water; the immediate surroundings are often unsanitary and hazardous; one or more family members may be victims of a debilitating disease; the children are likely to be malnourished; the family has experienced one or more infant deaths; the sons and daughters marry early; family planning has not been adopted and many women die in childbirth.

The adult members of the family are often illiterate. The children may never have been to a school or are likely to have dropped out. The family also remains uninformed in many other ways. Because of illiteracy, migration and increased isolation, the family members are unaware of existing opportunities and programmes meant for their benefit, and even if they do become aware, they are without the means to avail themselves of these opportunities. This partly explains the tendency towards so-called 'fatalism' among the family members.

The principal victims of these many poverties are the children, the women and the families in that order. The massive incidence of exploitative child labour and the multiple insults to womanhood are especially repulsive indicators of a situation of persistent deprivation.

The prevailing models of development – even those which spare a nod for the poor – typically bypass the poor and sometimes aggravate their plight. Recurring economic crises due to inefficiency, profligacy, non-accountability or the impact of external pressures exacerbate poverty. Constant transformations in the broader social, political, economic and informational environment render the existing fund of knowledge, resources and skills irrelevant for coping with a continuously changing and increasingly demanding environment. 'Structural adjustments' to new economic realities may help maintain vulnerable national macrosystems, but they invariably reduce the resources of and for the poor. Compensatory policy responses may limit the damage, yet they rarely amount to an antipoverty breakthrough. Growth strategies – indeed, economic growth itself – tend to discriminate against labour-intensive activities, thereby further skewing income distribution and accentuating poverty. Where positive results have been achieved, they have often occurred outside dominant socio-political structures, defying the deficiencies of these structures and bypassing the State.

Because of rapid urbanization, one-half of the world's population will soon be living in cities and towns. The changes generally associated with urbanization are also affecting rural life. Rootlessness, alienation and poverty in many forms are common features of life for hundreds of millions of urban migrants and slum dwellers.

The first report of the Indian National Commission on Urbanization offers a succinct description of the situation of the urban poor.

> We have spoken much of urban patterns and spatial planning. It is time we turn our attention to the people who inhabit our towns and cities, and here, without any doubt, that which is most clearly apparent and which causes the greatest anguish is the starkly visible poverty we see around us. It is arguably the worst pollution of all – manifest in the slums which dominate the townscape and in the mass of beggars, petty hawkers and casual workers struggling to eke out a living. The cities have wealth but the poor who live in them do not share in it. They service the city; they clean the houses of the rich and cook for them; they provide labour for factories and shops; they are the main carriers of goods, and yet they continue to be poor. The transference of poverty from a rural environment, where it is well spread out over space, to a city, where it is concentrated, presents perhaps the most horrifying images of independent India.[2]

The enormous problems facing the urban poor can be broken down into numerous conditions which combine to exacerbate their destitution and deepen their misery. Among these are low income, inadequate nutrition, limited education and shortages of skills. In addition there is an environmental poverty manifested in the lack or deficiency of public services, scarce housing, overcrowding, pollution and exposure to disease. The situation is further aggravated by a high level of psychosocial stress and insecurity that breeds depression and deviant and often violent social behaviour. A pervading hopelessness erodes ambitions and aspirations and thereby reduces the opportunities to demonstrate and apply one's abilities and energies for meaningful and constructive purposes.

The situation of the urban poor is an inevitable side-effect of the paths to development that many countries have chosen or have been forced to choose. The urban poor make cities work, but cities do not work for the poor. They are naked and alone and without even the flimsy safety nets which the most unfortunate rural communities can provide for their members.[3] This description can be extended to many cities, especially the rapidly growing megacities in the South. In these cities little is being done for the urban poor. They do not have access to affordable land for affordable housing, they are provided with few public amenities and they are unable to acquire sites to establish their small businesses.

The poor are accepted in the city mainly as a necessary evil, although without them the city would not function. The planning system has no place for them because urban masterplans aim at the creation of zoned residential areas and, at best, low-cost housing which is mostly beyond the reach of the very poor. Occasionally, political solutions are tried, but they are generally half-hearted and ineffective. For instance, leaseholds may be granted to people who have already helped themselves to open land and who would have survived on it anyway. For the truly poor, there is really nothing, nothing but themselves.

These telegraphic snapshots of the rural and urban poor and their many poverties need to be supplemented. Otherwise they may further a common attitude that the poor are poor because they deserve to be so. That would be to add insult to injury. The experience of economic poverty and the many other poverties is gruesome. These poverties limit choices and define important features of life, not least for children. Nonetheless, cultural meaning and social aspirations, though they may have to be adapted, remain major sources of energy and purpose for the parents and become so for the child as she passes through the various stages of childhood. This is often misunderstood, and economic poverty is interpreted as if poor people were devoid of all resources and abilities and lacked any purpose or meaning in their lives. This is a false and destructive view. It is obvious that we must never neglect or romanticize poverty. It is equally damaging if poverty is taken as an indication that the lives led by poor parents and their children are 'worthless'. Poverty is serious enough: it should not be aggravated by neglecting the dignity and resourcefulness which are often remarkably strong despite the cruelty of destitution.

Poverties in affluence

Many organizational processes in the world today are technology driven, be it through new production methods, new ways of generating energy or new communication systems. We must try to understand the effects of these on both children and adults and other massive transformations which societies have undergone during industrialization, urbanization, the expansion of the market economy and the accompanying atomization of social relations in many areas.

While poverty, ignorance, disease and environmental hazards still account for most of the problems in impoverished countries, similar problems are growing even in more well-off countries. The people in the 'North', not least the children, may have access to more abundant material and technological resources, but they tend to be increasingly isolated and alienated and more vulnerable to new forms of social and cultural poverties that make it difficult to cope or achieve a desirable quality of life. In illustrating such changes, an example from Sweden can also be used as a reminder of the globalization of some of the conditions of childhood. In the eyes of many observers, especially from the 'South', Sweden may appear free of problems, at least as far as children are concerned. Unfortunately, this is not so.

In Sweden, state and communal support for orphans and extremely destitute children has a long history, regardless of the quality or lack of quality of this support. The recognition of the state's broader responsibility towards children began to be articulated during the 1930s and 1940s. (Charitable organizations had, of course, been active much earlier.) The focus of the emerging official policy was not unlike that of many developing countries today. The ambition was, first, to reduce suffering and improve health and, second, to enhance skills through education.

A very far-sighted step was the establishment in the 1930s of an independent mother and child health service, which was publicly financed, but which was nonetheless actually and effectively community based. During the transition to a larger scale in all public sector activities during the 1950s and 1960s, the system was maintained as an independent and locally based service through the personal initiative of Olof Palme. 'This is something which works well,' said Palme. 'Let's not stifle it by "rationalizing" it.'[4]

During the 1960s the emphasis was on school reform and financial support for families, both measures being motivated by rapid industrialization. In the

1970s it was on encouraging women to participate in the labour force, partly for reasons connected to the labour market, partly as a response to insistent demands for gender equity. Childcare and maternity-paternity support were rapidly increased, although there was serious friction because of the lags between these changes and the movement of women into the workforce.

In the 1980s a general trend toward two-earner families, the disappearance of the housewife and the appearance of the daycare-centre child and the more isolated housechild was nearing a peak. Individualism, social atomization and alienation were growing. This process was accelerated by urbanization, immigration and the rapid and large-scale movement of people within the country for reasons of employment.

Around 1990 the pendulum swung back. Unemployment became a problem and segregation in housing increased, reflecting poor income distribution and the rising number of immigrants. The public support for two-earner families and one-parent households was reduced, although the economic need for such support was mounting. The social contract according to which the welfare state would assure the people significant material and social dividends is presently being replaced by a more limited and targeted safety-net approach.

A major outcome of the restructuring and subsequent shrinking of the labour market has been the concentration of poverty among women. This has sometimes been described as the 'pauperization of motherhood', since the most important factor in the poverty of women is the presence or absence of dependent children.

In a situation in which the supportive and complementary institutions and services of the state which offset the negative effects of the transformation of the labour market and other structural changes are being scaled back or closed down, there is little to fall back on. Politicians stress that neighbours ought to work together and point to the need to involve the elderly. However, in the era of privatization, politicians tend to forget that life on all levels has already been privatized and atomized to a large extent. In urban centres neighbours rarely know each other and, if they do, they are usually overworked and unable to participate in joint efforts. Grandparents seldom live in the same locality and the generations often have so little contact with each other that the creation of a new and supportive community for children, at least in the near future, is a rather utopian proposition.

This short and necessarily simplified summary of the case of Sweden demonstrates that the negative effects of major social transformations are not confined only to developing countries, but may be observed in most if not all countries. Although the actual forms these transformations take may differ, they invariably have a profound impact on the situation of children and the conditions of childhood. This renders it urgent to improve research, monitoring and data collection, so that the effects on children of these transformations can be captured and dealt with effectively in economic and social policy planning.

Laxmi

For an understanding of the many environments of the child, general information and a global view are no doubt necessary. Yet, many times these can obscure the human situations which they are meant to describe. The information produced through statistics and presented as representative averages must therefore be supplemented by individual snapshots and situational specifics. Wisely used, such pictures can serve as torchlights to help us understand the situation and the experiences of the individual, while at the same time revealing the many layers of causative factors at the international, national and local levels.

The following is a story about one child – a girl – and about the effects on her and on her life of the many environments of which she is part. While her story is only one among a number of possible stories, it also in many ways illustrates a worst case scenario. The girl, whose name is Laxmi, is but one child, but at the same time, like the drop of water in relation to the ocean, she is the many millions of children in similar situations around the world. This should not astonish us. A kindred thought is found in several philosophical traditions – perhaps most eloquently in *The Upanishads* of India – that the part contains and reflects all the properties of the whole. A life is a drop of the ocean that is thrown high by the waves but still carries within it all the properties of the whole of the ocean.

Laxmi's immediate surroundings consist of a mud hut – cold in winter, hot in summer – in one of the hundreds of villages in the tribal hills of Bihar in India. The terrain of the hills is difficult; the area is frequently hit by drought and floods and it is plagued by chronic poverty.

Like most people in the village, Laxmi's parents belong to a group which has been marginalized because of the caste system. Mahatma Gandhi was able to change the name of such people to 'Harijans', or 'the children of God'. Nonetheless, neither this nor decades of legal efforts to provide them with recognition and protection have broken down the age-old walls of discrimination and exclusion which surround them.

Public services in the village are few and of poor quality. The only source of safe drinking water is a single pump, which frequently breaks down; when this happens, a little stream which trickles into a walled-in pond must be used. The local health post is ill-equipped and often unattended. The teacher at the only school lives in another village and is regularly absent for days on end; school attendance is similarly haphazard.

A few buses provide contact with neighbouring villages and towns. Some of the local men read newspapers and meet to discuss the contents. Many people have radios, which usually blare music, but occasionally someone listens to reports on the comings and goings of the politicians in Patna, the capital city of Bihar. Most of the information is irrelevant to the villagers and does not penetrate their daily lives. Old people tell stories about earlier times when the landlords were hard and demanding, but nonetheless kept their part of a clearly unequal social contract and provided a minimum of security. The stories sound nostalgic sometimes, but the old people readily admit that there was suffering and exploitation then as now. Today the patron–client system has broken down, and more and more families are being left to fend for themselves.

Laxmi's first environment was her mother's womb. Microcosmic as this environment may have been, it had some of the basic characteristics of all the subsequent environments which Laxmi experienced. Like all of these, the first environment was very fragile and Laxmi's future was dependent on the forces which were giving shape to the environments – both the immediate ones and the larger ones – in which Laxmi's mother was living. These forces would determine if the child yet to be born would enter life with all the strength and potential which health offers or if she would awake into the world as a low birthweight, handicapped infant.

Laxmi was born a few weeks too early. Her umbilical cord was cut with a traditional knife of stone and covered with ashes from the hearth. She was underweight, but still full of life. Her first four months were taken up by sleeping and by feeding from her mother's breast. Laxmi's mother was soon hard at work once more, climbing the hills to seek fuel and fodder, which are becoming scarcer each year, walking to the village pump for water for drinking and washing, and spending endless hours over the wood stove or doing household chores. Sometimes Laxmi was taken along on her mother's back. However, most of the time she had to be left behind either alone or with a neighbour. This disrupted her feeding. Nonetheless, Laxmi was growing well, especially because she was protected by nutritious mother's milk.

The environments which awaited Laxmi were pitiless, demanding and full of risks. After only four months, the contending forces which made up her surroundings managed to break down her defences and disturb her health. Laxmi's father, a landless labourer, got drunk one night and beat her mother badly in a cruel display of poverty's chain of pain. Only 16, Laxmi's mother was still a child herself, and the shock made her unable to continue to breast-feed.

Two of the plates in Laxmi's human geology were clashing: the biological one, which provides her with food and protection, and the social one, which imposes poverty and gender inferiority. The shockwaves were serious. First, Laxmi was weakened by a few days of starving at the breast. Then, there were the loving but ignorant attempts to feed her from an improperly cleansed bottle containing a dangerous mixture of unsafe water and powdered milk from a borrowed package showing a 'consume before' date which was long past. Fortunately, the risks to Laxmi's life could be dealt with. The knowledge of the advantages of oral rehydration had already reached the village, and the local midwife had learned the value of supplementary feeding. Laxmi's father also pitched in by lessening his demands on his wife and offering a contribution of solidarity and love from one who had himself had little experience of either.

As Laxmi explored her surroundings in widening circles, old hazards were replaced by new ones: the danger of the careless disposal of fæces and other waste, the unclean water supply for drinking and washing, the constant infections and respiratory diseases emanating from an environment which carries an enormous bacterial overload, poor housing which cannot shelter her from the cold of winter, the rush through the village of a rabid dog and the exposed fireplace inside the hut.

The dangers are always there. When Laxmi was three, these dangers joined forces and struck once more, reaching for her life. It was late winter, and the diet of Laxmi's family was especially lacking in fruit and green vegetables. The protective lining of her respiratory system was weakened, as was her immune system. Her breath rate doubled in the space of 24 hours, but Laxmi had to fight alone, without the medical attention available not far away. The straightforward knowledge for recognizing the onset of pneumonia was not known to her parents. She managed to defend herself against this onslaught. Once more she survived, but once more the crisis took its toll on her energy, stunting her growth and restricting her important explorations of the surrounding world.

Soon Laxmi had a brother, and very soon her mother's stomach started to look rounded again.

'We need these children to help us work,' her father said.

'But we have no land to work,' his wife countered. 'They will drag us down and they will die.'

Within one month her mother's fears were proven right. Laxmi's brother contracted measles before the vaccination team had returned, and he died. Five months later another girl was born to Laxmi's parents.

'Bring us down they will: no son, and dowry twice over.' It was now the husband's turn to cry. The daily needs of food, fuel and clothing were growing. The overused and damaged environment offered the landless family little opportunity to fill these needs.

One day, the small family of four finally joined other neighbours in the sometimes hopeful, sometimes aimless, week-long walk to the nearby city in search of an environment which could support them. They had become ecological refugees.

We will leave Laxmi and her parents here without trying to guess their future. She is an individual child, but also an average child in the vast nation of children in the South and in pockets in the North. She is one child and at the same time scores of millions of children. All of the problems in her life are directly related to the nature of the many environments which surround her in smaller or larger circles. The manner in which her life will unfold will also depend on these environments and on the perceptions, knowledge and values which these environments contain and produce.

Notes and references

1. UNICEF (1995a).
2. NCU (1988), page 4.
3. For an extensive discussion, see Szanton Blanc (1994).
4. Personal communication to the author by Lisbet Palme.

Essay 2: Different times, different children

Major clusters of perceptions

Perceptions are reality and create reality. When they are firmly held, they express or give rise to deep, powerful, comprehensive and lasting beliefs, attitudes and behaviour.[1] They describe and maintain identities. They map and separate out the various components of our 'reality room', and they define our roles and our lifestyles and influence our views on human rights and obligations.

As far back as historical testimony can take us, perceptions about children, especially suffering children, have been based on views which can be described as 'charitable'. During the nineteenth century, missionaries preceding or accompanying the colonial expansion of the Western powers fostered an ambition to do 'good' by bringing back vivid stories about the hardship and suffering of peoples around the world. This helped strengthen the social and cultural basis for later charitable movements.

'Charity' denotes a wide range of activities which can be viewed as 'good' and worthy of support. Charitable initiatives are mainly recognizable by the intention of their supporters. They also draw strength from feelings of responsibility, kindness and compassion in the face of human suffering and from the identification of good causes with just causes. Further bolstered through the spread of the perception of the innocent and sacred child during the last century, a sense of charity became one of the key elements in the concern for children. Although there can be little doubt that charity is characterized by honourable ambitions, it is also clear that, if we take a closer look at the concept of 'charity', we discover that it is a very complex one. From the perspective of moral philosophy, Immanuel Kant even declared that charity ought to be regarded as obscene.

Charitable actions appeal to a sense of responsibility and help alleviate a sense of guilt. They are easily fuelled by images of suffering children, yet often they do not address the underlying causes of the problems of children. Thus, photos of children with sunken eyes in aged faces are frequently used to generate immediate child-centred actions, but they do not always lead to sustainable and long-lasting efforts to improve the essential support systems for the protection and betterment of children in all their many aspects. Because of these attributes, charitable initiatives in many ways represent the opposite of both the development approach and the child rights' perspective.

Charity as a benevolent concern for others is and will always be an intrinsic element in any well-intentioned effort to better the lot of those suffering from destitution and other ills. However, there is a risk that, once such well-intentioned action is carried out, it may leave the actors with the false impression that dealing with the immediate and obvious problems is the total solution. Moreover, because 'charitable' actions usually respond to urgent cries of distress, the rewards for the providers of charity – in terms of instant gratification – are seen as proof that the problems have indeed been solved, which is usually not the case. A basket of food might represent only a temporary relief in an existence on the margins of starvation and a carefully measured dose of antibiotics may only provide a short-lived respite in a continuing struggle for survival in an unhygienic and life-threatening environment. However, despite these shortcomings, it is equally important that charitable initiatives should not be ignored; nor should they be ridiculed or avoided. Charity has always been and will always remain a driving force of compassionate action. But it is a reasonable demand that the proponents of charity should explore the factors underlying the immediate suffering which triggers the charitable activities, together with the longer-term consequences of these activities. Without such precautions, some of the motivations for charitable initiatives are much less acceptable. Initiatives based mainly on the 'provider's' definition of the needs of the potential recipients can be – and frequently are – counterproductive. Such mistakes may seem clear-cut and therefore avoidable, but they are still all too common.

Another cluster of perceptions revolves around the 'emergency-humanitarian' approach to child suffering. Today, the principal goal of this approach is to save children's lives and protect them from hunger, disease and other afflictions caused by natural or man-made disasters. This approach differs from 'charitable' initiatives because of the sense of urgency, the focus of attention, the scale of the problems and the understandable inclination to concentrate on the immediate symptoms of suffering rather than on the causative factors. However, even in emergency situations complementary strategies can be applied. For example, the provision of food, shelter and medical assistance can be combined with efforts to make local schools more effective, and associations can be formed to identify and implement alternative survival and coping strategies and thus mobilize energies, confidence and resources which can help deter migration and the passive abandonment of one's life to the whims of unknown and unknowing outsiders.

A third cluster of perceptions about children has emerged more recently, which is represented by the development approach. The most fundamental and prominent argument for this approach is based on the idea that children ought to be allowed to grow to their full physical and intellectual potential. In a certain way then, the approach is similar to the human rights approach. Another significant rationale is the assumption that, through proper growth, children become more mature, useful and productive citizens as adults.

A fourth cluster of perceptions has been widely embraced in the last few decades. The term used by UNICEF to identify this cluster is 'child survival and development'. This consists of a combination of the elements of the emergency–humanitarian approach and of the development approach. Available technology is applied to combat the 'silent' emergencies caused by poverty, disease and a hazardous and abusive environment. The emphasis is on the need to use a 'cost-effectiveness' calculus to identify feasible goals and strategies which can be promoted despite financial constraints and other obstacles.

All the above clusters of perceptions exhibit an inclination to work as much as possible directly with children in dealing with their needs and problems.[2] Paradoxically, they also frequently share the disadvantage of viewing the suffering child as somehow isolated from the social and cultural space which he or she inhabits. They seem to thrive on an 'isolationist' view of the child in order to satisfy the need for immediate emotional gratification and sometimes also the desire to produce favourable statistics. This view seems to encourage goals and strategies which are very different from those which correctly emphasize the embeddedness of children and childhood in society and the constant interaction of children with society.

History and perceptions

The neglect of the historical perspective has left many people abandoned to the unquestioned belief that human betterment in general, as well as betterment for children, is universal in its goals and strategies. Although most of the following comments are focused on the history of the West, this should not be seen as weakening the argument that a historical perspective is important. In fact, precisely because of the Euro-centricism of the ideology of development and of the globalization strategies of the West, this focus is useful.

Without a historical perspective, the situation in one's own surroundings is seen as the norm and the situations of others as aberrations of the norm. The power of unquestioned values and rhetoric is rivalled only by the destructiveness of their insensitive application. Unaware that, throughout

Europe and North America well into modern times, infant and child mortality rates were generally very high, usually exceeding the worst levels in the least developed countries of today, and uninformed about the long history of child labour and the frequent abandonment of children in the West, well-intentioned practitioners may believe that these ills are confined mainly to those parts of the world where they now tend to be most frequent.

Without a comparative and historical perspective, this linkage to problems throughout the world – albeit at different moments in history – remains hidden. The lack of an honest historical perspective fosters on many levels a sense of inferiority in poor countries which is unjustified. It is also detrimental to the mutual confidence and respect necessary for the establishment of trusted partnerships for the betterment of children.

In the Western tradition, perceptions of children can be traced far back into history. Classical authors such as Aristotle, Seneca and Plutarch communicate sensitivity and a sympathetic understanding for the special conditions of children and childhood. Generally, however, the pictures of early death, routine abandonment (especially of girls), neglect, exploitation and abuse that have dimly reached us over the centuries are not pretty, although one might find it difficult to agree with Lloyd de Mause when he argues that 'the further back in history one goes, the lower the level of childcare and the more likely children are to [have been] killed, abandoned, beaten, terrorized and sexually abused'.[3]

Although imprecise and fragmented, there are some early statistics. They strongly suggest that infanticide was prevalent in the West, especially infanticide of girls and of children born out of wedlock. This practice seems to have been common until relatively recently, resulting in gross distortions in the ratios of females to males among populations.

One of the earliest of these 'demographic glimpses' comes from the ancient Greek city of Miletus on what is now the Aegean coast of Turkey. Of 79 families who gained citizenship in the city between 228 BC and 220 BC, there were 118 sons and 28 daughters.[4] Meanwhile, of the 600 families listed in second-century BC inscriptions in Delphi, only 1 per cent raised more than one daughter.[5]

In 374 AD, at roughly the same time that Christianity was being adopted as the state religion in the Roman Empire, infant killing was legally classified as murder. However, this had little effect on the customary practice of assisting all male offspring to survive, but only helping the first born daughter.[6] From the ninth and fourteenth centuries there is evidence in France of greatly distorted gender ratios, one source showing 172 adult males to 100 adult females.[7]

In contrast, some sculptural scenes, especially on sarcophagi, depict children with an affection that communicates effectively and passionately across the millennia. Descriptions of children and parental advice to children are also preserved in scores of private letters, mainly written by members of families of the elite. Otherwise, we know little from these times about children and their lives in the intimacy of families and households. As Cunningham points out:

> Ideas about childhood in the past exist in plentitude; it is not so easy to find out about the lives of children. There are sources which can tell us about their numbers in relation to adults, their life expectancy, the ages at which they were likely to start work and leave home and so on, but those seeking to recapture the emotional quality of the lives of children in the past encounter formidable hurdles.[8]

Nonetheless, child labour, harsh discipline, abandonment and abuse were clearly prominent features of childhood. In the fourteenth and fifteenth centuries such hardships led, particularly in Italy and France, to 'public projects' aimed at children. These included foundling hospitals such as the Spedale degli Innocenti in Florence.[9]

The French Revolution is considered a milestone in the recognition of human rights. However, in the constitutional documents produced by the new republic, the rights and obligations of full citizenship were recognized only for adult males; women, children and the mentally ill were excluded. Indeed, only later, following the rise of the movement for the abolition of slavery during the first decades of the nineteenth century, did the plight of working children and abused children begin to attract attention.

In the meantime, by the end of the eighteenth century the size of the bourgeoisie had become significant throughout Europe. New wealth was being created which had to be maintained and transferred among family members and augmented through financially attractive alliances. Perceptions about children and childhood which emphasized protection, isolation and discipline became more common, as did the 'idolization' of children and the view of the child as 'innocent' or 'sacred'. Regardless of what may have been the linkages between these parallel changes, the conflict between attitudes of reverence and a desire for discipline points to a complex and difficult social and emotional climate for children even when material poverty was not an immediate problem.

With the expansion of industrialization came a new motivation to give greater attention to children and to improve their education: children were the generation of the future, or, more accurately, 'the workforce of tomorrow'. Among the growing bourgeoisie, new riches and consequent interest in planning for the intergenerational transfer and preservation of resources provided other incentives for an increased concern for children and childhood.

During the Crimean War the public, through the emerging 'global' communications media of the telegraph and the newspaper, were made aware of the horrible conditions among victims of war, thereby favouring the conviction that wounded soldiers had a right to special attention and protection. The seeds of the Red Cross and Red Crescent societies were thus planted, and people generally began to show more concern for victims of disasters, whether man-made or natural. This represented a sea change in the evolution of human morality that eventually also fostered a transformation in perceptions about suffering children and their right to protection.

The growth of public concern for children

In England during the nineteenth century, socially conscious authors, like Charles Dickens, and compassionate philanthropists fighting against rampant and exploitative child labour, like Lord Shaftesbury and Robert Barnardo, were instrumental in initiating a public debate on the situation of children. A political culmination of sorts was achieved in 1889, when the British Parliament adopted the Prevention of Cruelty to and Better Protection of Children Act. The member of Parliament promoting the new legislation expressed his anxiety in the House of Commons that children should be given 'the same protection that we give under the Cruelty of Animals Act and the Contagious Diseases Act for Domestic Animals', which had been adopted by Parliament 76 years earlier, in 1823.[10]

During these years, the public debate was often torn between romantic perceptions of the 'sacred' child and advocacy for the application of sterner methods both to protect children and to educate them. The special nature of childhood was thus being underlined, and the borders of the age of a child, a young person and adults were being more broadly defined and recognized. Even a new type of literature offering advice to parents on how to treat children and deal with child-related problems began to appear. A seminal work was the two-volume *The Century of the Child* written by Ellen Key and first published in Swedish in 1900.[11] The book was eventually translated into 13 languages and appeared in 337 different editions and reprints, the latest in 1990. Although the book was not 'scientific' in any formal sense, since Key drew her ideas mainly from literature and other non-science sources, it focused clearly on a framework of childhood that had been socially and psychologically conditioned. Key's work has had a decisive influence directly and indirectly on the study of childhood as a social and cultural construct.[12]

Efforts to deliver humanitarian aid to the combatants during the First World War and the suffering of children in the aftermath of the conflict were the inspiration for the establishment of the international Save the Children movement. Eglantyne Jebb, the Englishwoman who founded Save the Children, had defied the law on the grounds that there was no such thing as an 'enemy child'. Her dream was to translate the initiative into a binding international agreement. Thus in 1923, Jebb, with the help of the International Committee of the Red Cross and the Save the Children International Union, drafted the first declaration on the rights of the child. The document was adopted a year later by the League of Nations.

'Mankind owes to the child the best that it has to give,' states the document.[13] It was a simple document with only five clauses. It demanded for the child the means for material, moral and spiritual development, special help for the hungry, sick, handicapped and orphaned, the first right to relief in times of distress, training to earn a living, protection from exploitation, and an upbringing which would instil in the child a sense of duty towards society.

The enormous suffering at the time in the newly established Soviet Union and the humanitarian mobilization led by Fritjof Nansen had a startling and lasting effect on many concerned people all over the world. Similar warning bells were being sounded because of the plight of children during the conflicts in Ethiopia and Spain in the latter part of the 1930s. Growing awareness of the victimization of children by internal and external forces in the colonies under the control of the European powers slowly started to generate concern for the peoples of the countries of Asia and Africa.

The Second World War was another watershed. Despite forceful political opposition, spirited groups in England founded Oxfam to relieve the suffering among the children of Greece. In the wake of the war, the United Nations Relief and Rehabilitation Agency (UNRRA) was established as a multilateral agency to ease the tremendous hardships of entire populations in Europe and Eastern Asia. Much of its emergency work concentrated on children and their immediate needs. UNRRA was succeeded by the United Nations Children's Fund (UNICEF), which provided first a temporary and later, from 1953, a permanent framework for international cooperation for children. UNICEF realized from the beginning that communication, information and efforts to broaden and deepen the debate on children and their welfare would have to play a major role in any strategy for improving the situation of children.

The outspoken advocacy for children during the Biafran conflict and the worldwide mobilization generated by the International Year of the Child in 1979 were milestones in the intensification of concern for children. The publication of the yearly UNICEF report *The State of the World's Children* beginning in 1981 and later of the series *The Progress of Nations* reflected the same conscious strategy of stimulating further debate on betterment for children.

Meanwhile, the coverage of the theoretical debate was also expanding. Among the major overviews of childhood as a construct which has evolved over the centuries was Philippe Ariès's *L'enfant et la vie familiale sous l'ancien régime*, which was published in 1960 and which quickly became well known both inside and outside history circles.[14] One of Ariès's main theses is that a well-defined 'childhood' first emerged in Europe only during the eighteenth century. He argued that before that time and in contrast with classical times, when a clear distinction was drawn between children and adults, the transition moved directly from infancy to dependent minor, who was treated as though he were a small adult.

In the 1980s the historical approach to perceptions about children and the nature of childhood was subjected to wide-ranging criticism. According to this criticism and quite contrary to the ideas put forward by Ariès:

> The history of child-parent relations ... was marked not by dramatic change, but by little or no change at all; parents by and large had always loved their children. The family was a constant in history, well capable of defending itself in its nuclear form against the intrusions of church or state.[15]

Ariès was criticized for having ignored evidence which supported the view that there were perceptions and conceptualizations of childhood during the Middle Ages. He was also upbraided for less than reliable historical research methods.

The pendulum of opinion had swung so far that, by the end of 1980, the outlook seemed to be taking hold that nothing had really ever changed very much after all, at least not in how children had been perceived throughout history. This view was, however, immediately challenged, and today, only a decade later, most historians would probably agree that perceptions about childhood have undergone substantial changes in the course of history, although the emotional affection and an ambition to care may have formed the 'normal' foundation for parent-child relationships at all times and in all cultures.

In his most recent work, Cunningham describes what he argues is the latest phase in the ongoing historical process of 'constructing and reconstructing' perceptions about children and childhood in Western societies.

> The peculiarity of the late twentieth century, and the root cause of much present confusion and angst about childhood, is that a public discourse which argues that children are persons with rights to a degree of autonomy is at odds with the remnants of the romantic view that the right of the child is to be a child. The implication of the first is a fusing of the worlds of adult and child, and of the second the maintenance of separation.[16]

Another dominant feature in the recent debate has been identified by Zelizer in *Pricing the Priceless Child*. She points to the 'sharp contradiction ... between the public and the private value of children.'[17]

Reviewing the situation in North America, Grubb and Lazerson, in an earlier book, reach a similar conclusion.

> Americans fail their children.... The saccharine myth of America as a child-centred society, whose children are its most precious natural resource, has in

practice been falsified by our hostility to other people's children and our unwill-
ingness to support them.[18]

Parents may spend lavishly and irrationally on their own children, but their
altruism is transformed into miserliness when it comes to public programmes. The 'sacred' child is a luxury commodity restricted to the private
sphere. Children in need of public support must show in economic terms that
they are worthy of economic investment. This is a widespread attitude in the
public debate on children and childhood. Children are worthy causes, but
not worthy citizens. Likewise, there is a universal tendency to identify and
evaluate children and childhood not on their own terms, but relative to the
adult members of society. Such one-sided comparisons understandably and
predictably lead to the characterization of children as biologically and
socially immature and thus inferior to adults who, by definition, are the
yardstick of maturity.

Elise Boulding has pointed to another factor which contributes to perceptions that children are helpless and, consequently, inferior. In *Children's
Rights and the Wheel of Life*, she argues that the doctrine of the helplessness of
the young and the aged has been developed in those particular circles most
concerned with the rights of individuals.

> The convenience of age-segregated social patterns, initially evolved in the West to
> further the education of the young, ensured that contradicting information from
> human development research about substantial unused human capacity and abil-
> ity in the earliest and latest years of life did not penetrate to policymaking circles.
> What began as a humanitarian concern for the weak has resulted in a depersonaliz-
> ing and devaluing of individual capacity in the young and the old through a
> doctrine of protection that has converted persons in these categories from subjects
> to objects of social concern.[19]

Boulding's engaged voice brings home with rare strength and vibrancy the
fact that the history of childhood to a great extent is a history of exclusion. No
matter what changes in analysis, theories and practice we may consider for
the betterment of the conditions of children, this process must be reversed.

Notes and references

1. Geertz (1973), page 94.
2. See Rädda Barnen (1995), page 12.
3. de Mause (1976), page 1.
4. de Mause (1976), page 22.
5. de Mause (1976), page 22.
6. de Mause (1976), page 28.

7. de Mause (1976), page 39.
8. Cunningham (1995), page 2.
9. The extensive archives of the Spedale degli Innocenti in Florence are presently being analysed. Comparative case studies are being produced during this process. See Corsini and Grieco (1991) and Corsini and Viazzo (1993).
10. Pinchbeck and Hewitt (1973), page 625, cited in Therborn (1993).
11. Key (1900).
12. See, for example, Stafseng (1993).
13. Black (1986), page 199.
14. See the English edition: Ariès (1962).
15. Cunningham (1991), page 2.
16. Cunningham (1995), page 190.
17. Zelizer (1985), page 216.
18. Grubb and Lazerson (1982), pages 51ff.
19. Boulding (1979), page 2.

Essay 3: Commonalities and variations in perceptions about children

When we discuss children and childhood, we have to touch every corner and every aspect of human reality in politics, the economy, health, education and the environment, as well as deal with all the many institutions and administrative structures devised by man to oversee production, reproduction, the control of resources, the organization of power and the accumulation and application of knowledge.

In order to be able to identify and manage issues relating to childhood we also need to examine questions about the similarities and the differences in the cultural and social manifestations of childhood throughout the world. It is quite astonishing that this area of inquiry has been so poorly covered in social and cultural studies. Admittedly, socialization is much discussed, especially in terms of psychology. However, apart from the now ageing books by Mead and Wolfenstein and by the Whitings, and the more recent ones by Wagner and Stevenson and by Kessel and Siegel, there has not been much serious theoretical effort in this direction.[1]

Nonetheless, there are signs that a change may be under way. Decades of policies and programmes carried out by progressive nations, voluntary organizations and UNICEF have begun to achieve results, especially in the areas of child survival and health. Since the International Year of the Child in 1979, advocacy for children has intensified. The Convention on the Rights of the Child has propelled these concerns and efforts decisively into the political debate over human rights. The follow-up of the World Summit for Children – the national plans of action, the endeavour to foster improvements in budgetary allocations and official development assistance for children, and the call for 'children first' – are illustrative of the attempts to translate into political action the ethical energy which has been stirred.

Efforts to construct and strengthen the theoretical and empirical underpinnings for a fresh approach to children and childhood are also mounting. Since 1981, UNICEF's yearly report *The State of the World's Children* has been drawing the world's attention to child-related issues.[2] Most developing countries are now producing regular reports on the situation of children within their borders. The European project, Childhood as a Social Phenomenon, represents a major attempt to adopt a comprehensive method for understanding childhood in various national and cultural contexts.[3] Two recent publications make important, concrete proposals on the way to proceed. One is *Toward a Children's Agenda*, the contribution of Save the Children (UK) to the Social Summit in 1995.[4] Another is the draft of a proposal for a European strategy for children which is being prepared for formal adoption by the Council of Europe.[5] Although the one is a policy paper drawing on recent studies of children and childhood issues, and the other the draft outline of a regional policy, there is in the two documents a surprising amount of agreement about the views on children and childhood and the relationship between childhood and adult society, as well as in the general recommendations for changing and strengthening policies for children.

Academic attention is also becoming more focused on issues linked with childhood. The works of Bronfenbrenner and the recent publication of *Constructing and Reconstructing Childhood* by James and Prout, together with a series of commentaries on various aspects of the Convention on the Rights of the Child, are indications of a growing interest.[6] However, these attempts are still rather feeble in their effect on the dominant discourse in social science, economics and politics. In fact, the work towards a deepened understanding of children and childhood has only just begun.

The environment of childhood

Every society recognizes a defined period of time in an individual's life as childhood. As a category within society, childhood can be defined as the combined set of socially and culturally instituted arrangements for the identification, protection and gradual transformation of children into socially defined adults in parallel with their biological growth. Childhood is a framework for the organization and location of the various social spaces in which children participate and through which they pass. Here, we find preparations for handling birth and for the acceptance and identification of the newborn, nursing and care for young children and then training and early participation in defined areas of adult life. Childhood is therefore, as Qvortrup indicates, a 'permanent social category' and not merely a transient phase of life.[7] Qvortrup suggests that childhood is 'a particular and distinct' structural form comparable with social class, which 'gains its defining characteristics by what the members of childhood … are doing and by the position childhood is assigned by other and more dominant groups in society'.[8]

To compare childhood and social class may be tempting. However, the variations among the members of childhood in societies are often large and are dependent on factors which are sometimes quite distinct from those involved in the generation and differentiation of classes. They may also reflect a great many contrasts in the 'adulthoods' surrounding children. Childhood is indeed very far removed from Weber's classic definition of 'class' as the categories or groups of people with similar life chances which are clearly unlike those of other groups in the society.

Nonetheless, Qvortrup's conceptual proposal is helpful because it emphasizes that childhood is a permanent and universal social formation in which a significant part of human life is experienced. Childhood is best described as a social and cultural category within the life cycle that guides, conditions, supports and legitimizes children's participation in, and exploration of, physical, social and cultural spaces. This takes place within structural forms which are specifically arranged for members of childhood, such as educational facilities, where children participate with other members of society, including the family, the household, the neighbourhood, the local community and organizations involving some or all of these.

Public and sometimes official rhetoric is changing towards 'children first' and children's rights. This should be welcomed. However, it does not mean that there is now a consensus that children are important. In reality, the situation has not changed so much. The rhetoric cannot hide the fact that the advances achieved thus far are very small in comparison to the obligations which adult society places on children and in view of the widespread disregard and violation of even the most elementary rights of children.

To redirect the debate on children and improve on our analysis and understanding of childhood, it is important that the issue of the obligations of children be openly debated and honestly addressed. Like rights, these obligations pose difficult philosophical and legal questions. It is astonishing that an overwhelming share of attention – even in progressive circles – is devoted to the issue of rights. This bias distorts our understanding and weakens the analysis of the issue of rights and consequently damages the promotion and the implementation of children's rights. One possible explanation of this potentially dangerous situation is that children's rights can be meaningfully discussed and understood in terms of human and civil rights generally. The issue of children's obligations, however, cannot be dealt with through reference to the nature of the obligations of adult and reasonably equal partners or by simplistic reference to contractual relationships based on a balance between rights and obligations.

Indeed, there are clear differences between the rights and obligations of children and those of adults.[9] We must realize that, although children, especially small children, cannot be regarded as having individual obligations in the same way adults can, children and childhood do collectively bear tremendous obligations. Indeed, children are brought into the world as a result of a series of expectations, even obligations, that adult society places on them. Children are required to furnish emotional gratification and provide recognition and respect for their procreators, male and female. They are expected to offer support and assistance to parents and other caregivers, at least in the long term. Other sets of obligations placed on children from the beginning demand that children learn, go to school and become educated. Furthermore, adult society establishes rules so that the physical, biological, mental and social growth of children is assured. The ultimate purpose of these obligations is to guarantee that children acquire the maturity and skills – once more defined by adult society – to be able to engage fully in the social and cultural and eventually the biological reproduction of society.

This outline of the obligations of children exposes the dangers of viewing children's rights in isolation as if they were some benevolent gift of adult society to its minors. The issue of rights must be placed next to the issue of the significant obligations demanded of children individually and of childhood collectively, obligations which easily dwarf even the most generous inter-pretation of the rights listed in the Convention on the Rights of the Child.

The argument is not that children should be freed from obligations; many obligations represent ethical imperatives and provide desirable opportuni-ties to foster growth and future strength. Neither is the argument that children ought to have rights because they have obligations. Like other human beings, children have certain inalienable rights without regard to the existence of obligations. Rather, the argument is that, if the surrounding context of broad obligations demanded of children is not recognized and correctly understood, the promotion of children's rights will suffer.

Childhood is continuously interacting with other components in the total web of human reality. Through this interaction, children are in their own specific way not only crucial for the production, reproduction and sustain-ability of human life, but are in a very real sense also co-builders of the social and cultural structures which make up our communities and societies.

These comments point to an overriding postulate which must guide both theory and practice in the effort to improve the situation of children: the principle of the fundamental 'embeddedness' of children and childhood in society and thereby in economy, government and culture. This principle represents a substantial advance on the hitherto dominant perception of the child as isolated, whether because idolized or neglected.

The principle has important implications. For example, it means that, if the fight against poverty, inequity and injustice is not vigorously pursued, betterment for children will not be forthcoming. If technologies are in-humane and ineffective, if unemployment is rampant, or if the organization of human life on local and national levels is inadequate or oppressive, children will suffer. The principle of embeddedness will also transform our inquiries into the situation of children and affect our understanding and identification of the problems facing children. This in turn will influence the selection of strategies designed to improve the conditions in which children live.

From now on, the child must be regarded as a subject, a member, a citizen, an actor and a co-builder of society. This will require heightened efforts to focus on the child in her own right and it will require that the many environments of the child be mapped and analysed in order to understand more clearly the relevant patterns of dependency and interdependency.

This principle reflects the essence of the child's situation and represents a basis for theoretical, ethical and practical enquiry. The principle of embeddedness incorporates a view of the nature of the relationship between children and their many social and cultural environments. It should be useful in correcting the undesirable and distorting effects of the competing perceptions which tend to isolate, marginalize and trivialize children and their problems.

The environment of culture

The so-called 'cultural sector' is not a separate compartment of reality: it is one aspect of our perception of reality. One could consider it an organizing principle.[10] What we call 'society' is basically a summary of our attempts to deal with the organizational and structural ordering of our collective lives. In similar fashion, 'culture' covers our efforts to achieve a logical and meaningful interpretation of our common experiences. This is very different from the 'normal' interpretation of culture that tends to regard 'cultures' as separate entities surrounded by identifiable boundaries. Equally misleading is the practice of specifically locating cultural 'activities' in spheres, such as literature, art, music and theatre, which are managed by especially gifted and trained art professionals.

Our culture influences the way we interpret the situations in which we are actors and the actions we regard as socially acceptable. Our culture suggests the material and non-material goals we choose for our personal lives. It helps determine the kind of impression which we aim to communicate in each specific situation, as well as generally, and it offers common signs, symbols and metaphors through which we can exchange thoughts with each other.[11] Thus, culture is the knowledge we share within a community or within a society. It is the constellation of images about the world – the way we think it is and the way we think it ought to be – and about ourselves – who we are and who we aspire to be – which is transferred, generation to generation, through the medium of childhood and there, among the children, altered and reinterpreted.

What comes first, culture and values which guide behaviour or behaviour which gives rise to values? These two sides of a single question have often been seen as contradictory, one labelled 'idealism' and the other 'material-ism'. Most attempts to reconcile the two have been blocked by a simplistic 'either-or' approach. The seeming contradiction between the two views is, however, not so difficult to resolve.

The behaviour, the technology and the modes of production which helped groups of people survive in an acceptably efficient manner gave rise to certain values. Once such values had been recognized and established they came to play an important part in the organization of social life, in the interpretation of the meaning and purpose of life and, in turn, in the identifi-cation of norms guiding behaviour. Clearly, 'cultural' perceptions, including values, are not vague attitudes which can simply be discarded overnight. Values which codify and legitimize behaviour in crucial areas related to the purpose and meaning of life are extremely stubborn. An African house may not have partitions or internal walls in brick and mortar, but the division among the spaces in these houses and the right to use these spaces are never-theless recognized, understood and respected, probably more intensely because they are firmly present in the mind. In this way, perceptions are creative of reality. A story can bring this home much better than can any analysis.

Miriam Were, a young Kakamega woman from Kenya, was educated by the collective efforts of family and village members.[12] She eventually became a medical doctor. When she had finished her studies abroad, she wished to express her appreciation for the support she had received from her com-munity. So, she returned to her village in Kenya to try to deal with the funda-mental problems of child health that existed there. She knew that parasite infestation among children was a major problem and that the disciplined use of latrines could be an effective solution, but her information was received in the village with scepticism and then rejection.

'You are another one destroyed by the books,' she was told. The local theory was that children were born with parasites and that moral faults of the parents related to the rituals for dealing with ancestors caused this destruc-tive health problem. The traditional remedy was to collect the fæces of the children and cover them with leaves according to the ritual instruction of the moral leader of the community. Nonetheless, Were continued to teach and preach her views until, finally, she became quite depressed, having realized that generations would pass before the message in her textbooks could be translated into practice in her village. She was determined to do something, so she called a village meeting.

'Why don't we try the following,' she said to the gathering. 'You are worried and you spend a lot of time identifying the condition of the fæces of your children. And then you spend time and money to get advice on ways to deal with the problem. Let's deal with the problem together once and for all. Let's dig collective graves and see to it that children always, or as often as possible, defecate in those graves. Perform the prescribed rituals on every occasion, regardless of the situation, and both the child and you will be safe.'[13]

Over a period of one year and a half, with minimal support from UNICEF, Miriam single-handedly convinced 42 000 households, representing approximately 240 000 people, to raise the use of latrines from 3 per cent to 97 per cent. Two 'cultures' had met and reached agreement and the combination resulted in a dramatic improvement in children's health. Together, the two cultures constructed a bridge between local and global knowledge, between local and global practice and between local and global values.

The environment of values

Although biases are often politely and carefully concealed, beliefs, values and a religious or spiritual perspective are commonly regarded as a form of knowledge which is less relevant than the economic and sociological principles guiding the prevalent approach to development. The idea that they may represent different rather than competing insights is rarely considered.[14]

Occasionally, in order to facilitate the promotion of various development programmes, so-called experts discover an interest in 'traditional' or religious values. They wish to overcome what they perceive as an obstacle to development. In many cases this desire is genuine, for it is aimed at modifying culturally and religiously accepted views which foster serious abuses of human rights. Nonetheless, in general, we ought to view spiritual values and religious convictions as important expressions of a dimension of human reality which is at least as real as the tangible and quantifiable physical, technological and social aspects. Indeed, the spiritual and religious dimension may sometimes even be perceived as more real than the 'tangible' dimension. Sometimes it is necessary to redirect mistaken beliefs and superstitions, but more often it is necessary to learn to understand and respect differing world views, the religions of which they are part and the ethical constructs to which they give rise. An example from Sri Lanka may help illustrate this point.

The international adoption of children is a global phenomenon. Sometimes, the 'adoptions' are exploitative and abusive, and children have been treated as commodities and sold for export by unscrupulous middlemen, often with the acquiescence of bribed officials. Other times, the adoptions are the result of a serious search process aimed at identifying children and adoptive parents who are 'compatible' and have a good chance to build a lasting and beneficial relationship.

In the 1970s, social workers and representatives of voluntary child-activist groups from Sri Lanka were brought together with their counterparts from Sweden.[15] The triggering factor was a press campaign in Sri Lanka which was being conducted against international adoption, however needy the child. The campaign had very significant emotional overtones because it was motivated by a strong distaste of the country's perceived abandonment of its children. One sensed that international adoption was regarded as an admission of poverty, underdevelopment and neglect, and that this was wounding the national pride.

On the other hand, the Swedish side was experiencing a very negative reaction towards what it considered a callous attitude towards disadvantaged children. To the Swedes the situation seemed clear. There were two sets of needs: the lack of a home among the abandoned or orphaned children who were sliding toward a life of poverty and neglect and the pain of childless couples in Sweden who desired nothing more than to offer their homes to children. If a meeting ground could be found for these two sets of needs, the negatives on both sides of the equation could be eliminated.

As the discussions evolved, some of the reasons for the energy and the strength of the Sri Lankan opposition to international adoptions became quite tangible. In the Sri Lankan view the Swedish equation omitted important facts. However materially poor life in Sri Lanka might be, the Buddhist tradition was the only one which could satisfy the need for cultural and spiritual identity. Sri Lankans could not accept responsibility for denying a child, whatever its situation, the opportunity of liberation from the 'imprisoning circle of returns' that was reincarnation. Because this liberation could be achieved only in a Buddhist environment, such an environment was essential for the child despite the obvious benefits which the Swedish welfare state could provide. The Sri Lankans also argued that many of the child's needs as perceived by the Swedes were either the needs of the adoptive parents or they had been produced by a consumer society and were therefore artificial and detrimental. The Swedes could not understand these arguments, much less accept them. The contact was broken off. Eventually, Sri Lanka's rules for foreign adoption were considerably tightened.

The case is a concrete example of a profound clash between the 'modern' world views of outsiders and the essential values among local people who are meant to 'benefit' from a programme designed to alleviate problems among destitute children. Clearly, a better understanding of the importance in the total 'reality room' of the dimension of firmly held beliefs and of perceptions of the meaning and purpose of children and childhood might have led to effective, relevant and sustainable solutions to the problems of destitute children.

Cultural values and universal rights

Culturally and religiously determined perceptions must be understood and respected. However, serious ethics and genuine values must be distinguished from distortions of these which have been nourished mainly for social and economic gain or for political reasons. The quintessentially religious must be differentiated from the more mundane dressed up in religious raiment. The Jesuit economist and scholar William F. Ryan has described this complex and often bewildering mix in the following way.

> Cultural values, including religions, prompt people to mobilize for certain achievements. Religions were born largely on values – justice, love, security and charity. Then they proceeded to stratification, codes and covenants with the divine to enhance their influence. Somehow, somewhere, sometime, these codes then became rigid laws and customs which are taken in and of themselves as values. The laws and customs have become the 'golden calves'![16]

It is obvious that the neglect of culture, religion and the dimensions of value and meaning and the distortions and misunderstandings which this neglect creates are serious. However, recognition and respect for cultures and values are not the same as acceptance.

Following the near universal ratification of the Convention on the Rights of the Child, the resolution of conflictual relationships between cultural perceptions and negotiated and recognized universal norms has taken on new significance and urgency. Alston has summarized the challenge succinctly in his discussion of the principle of the best interests of the child.

> Just as culture is not a factor which should be excluded from the human rights equation, so too must it not be accorded the status of a metanorm which trumps rights. There are many cultural practices which, by human rights standards, are difficult if not impossible to reconcile.... There are also many ... cases in which cultural arguments continue to be used today to justify the denial of children's rights. They include arguments designed to defend the full range of practices relating to female circumcision, to justify the non-education of lower class or caste children, or to justify the exclusions of girls from educational and other opportunities which would make them less sought after in marriage.[17]

Cultural variations and universal commonalities among children

Generalizations and the abstractions they engender can lead to a false universalism. People who do not doubt their superiority regard themselves as 'universal' and therefore without race or ethnicity. In the same way men sometimes perceive gender as applying only to women. As Frances Olsen has pointed out, 'The claim of unsituatedness is made by and on behalf of those with power.'[18]

The same tendency is evident in the debate on children. When children are treated as though they were devoid of context, there is a danger that the guiding perceptions against which they will be measured will be those about the children of the powerful – probably male – American, Japanese or European. This raises some important questions. When can children be regarded only as children and therefore treated as one group? Under which circumstances are children different as children?

As Betty Caldwell points out, the visible (and audible) differences among children from various cultural backgrounds sometimes obscure the features held in common.[19] The differences are not absolute, and the variations not endless. 'Each child is to some extent like all children, to some extent like some children, and to some extent like no other child.'[20]

Caldwell suggests that there are at least three sets of universals that can be identified among children: they have similar needs and rights; they go through basically the same stages of physical and social growth; and the goals of the interactions among children and the larger society are essentially the same. In these ways each child is like all children.

However, common features among and within specific cultures are likely to influence the conditions in which children live and the nature of their childhood.[21] These include the organization of the physical and temporal environment, the availability of toys and play materials, parental involvement with the child in teaching and learning, and the provision of variety in daily experience. Having or not having access to clusters of these 'offerings' will affect the growth of the child. Children growing up in similar environments are, of course, more like each other than are those who have significantly different patterns of home experience. Similarities in these patterns help to identify groups of children who will in important ways share characteristics with some other children.

Finally, there are ways in which each child is like no other child, a unique individual in terms of genetic potential, sensory capacity, history of reinforcement, ability to relate to other people, energy level, temperament, interests and motivation.[22]

It is essential that we bear in mind the similarities and the differences if we wish to sharpen our tools for exploring the nature of the social and cultural 'spaces' of children during the various phases of childhood. Caldwell's commonsense approach provides a useful classification of the various levels and contexts within children's environments that can help us to identify and understand differences as well as similarities in the abilities and behaviour of children. A sensitivity towards the variations and common features in our perceptions about children needs to be fostered. Without such a sensitivity, there will be little opportunity to erect the bridges of understanding which are so necessary for the precise identification of problems, the communication of information about these problems and advocacy in the effort to find solutions. This sensitivity is equally important for the establishment of a global movement for the betterment of children, since this movement requires a solid foundation of knowledge, supportive perceptions and guiding values to address the universal needs of children and the social and cultural variations in these universal needs.

In the case of a girl child in a poor family in India, the need for protection against disease and for the provision of parental care and adequate nutrition is truly universal and makes the child like all other children. In addition, in South Asia, as in other parts of the world, there is often a strongly held belief that females should play a subservient role and that this role should be oriented towards reproduction. This renders our girl child like some other children who are living in cultural environments especially prone to violations of the rights to dignity and to protection of girls and women.

We must realize that cultural perceptions are not vague variations in attitudes which can be easily changed or eliminated through effective public awareness campaigns. This is especially true for those perceptions which 'codify' and legitimize behaviour in crucial areas related to the purpose and meaning of life and the way to organize life. It is worth repeating that perceptions are reality and create reality.

Among the rural Oromo of Western Ethiopia, children under three or four years of age are regarded with tolerance and offered support by both women and men. They enjoy a great deal of leeway and 'freedom' within and around the space of the home. The smaller children are active, playful and noisy. In this they resemble children of suburban America who are noisy, competitive and lively. In sharp contrast, during subsequent stages of childhood among the Oromo, children are guided to distinguish carefully between emerging male and female roles and are subject to increasing discipline and growing responsibilities, for the girls in relation to their mothers, siblings and household chores, and for the boys in regard to the work of men outside the house. It is as if playfulness and 'childishness' disappear all of a sudden. During moments of leisure it is common to find children of pre-puberty age doing nothing. While outsiders often choose to see such behaviour as a sign of apathy, malnutrition or fatigue, the children and their parents value such behaviour as a sign of 'being in control' and 'being at peace'. This behaviour reflects values and role models which are very different from those in Western societies, where the active, even hyperactive, child is considered healthy, happy and a symbol of joy.[23]

Dominant perceptions are usually strongly codified in language. In the Bangla language there is a word, *shishu*, which, like the concept of 'child' employed in the Convention on the Rights of the Child, can be applied to both boys and girls. However, it only refers to children of pre-school age. For subsequent stages of childhood and youth, distinct concepts for 'boy' and 'girl' are used. These correspond to the distinct sets of perceptions and social goals that are applied to boys and to girls. Many perceptions about boys have little or no relevance to the perceptions about girls, and vice versa.

'The use of a gender neutral word to describe youth up to the age of 18 reifies childhood in a way which is meaningless in Bengali culture.' Consequently, it is difficult to find support for arguments that standards for boys should pertain to girls and that only in this way can discrimination be avoided. Furthermore, older children who 'are already burdened with heavy responsibilities and workloads ... are no longer seen as shishu and are denied protection.'[24]

These briefly condensed cases illustrate the importance of awareness not only of the existence of variations in perceptions, but also of the need to respect the strength, the reality and the legitimizing function of some of these perceptions. Indeed, cultural perceptions must be taken much more seriously than they usually are both when they are supportive of children's rights and when they conflict with these rights. Professional experts (who by definition are outsiders) tend to dismiss local, institutionalized perceptions as beliefs or prejudices of little relevance or consequence. The opposite is true. The roads which perceptions map, the bridges which they build and the walls which they erect are strong. This means that efforts to bring about change whenever cultural views conflict with universally negotiated and adopted rights need to have a similar 'strength' and 'legitimacy'.

Our girl child in India is finally – like all children – in some respects like no other child. Her inherent potential and the way she responds to the opportunities and constraints emanating from her many environments are specific to her. The strengthening of certain crucial aspects of these environments and the reduction of some of the obstacles which stand in the way of a meaningful and fulfilling life are the very basis for the obligations of adult society and national and international communities towards the individual child. Although the strategies for such betterment cannot be individualized and the needs confronted ought to be the needs of the many, the overriding goal in these efforts and the ultimate indicator of progress is the better life for each and every child.

Notes and references

1. Mead and Wolfenstein (1955), Whiting and Whiting (1975), Wagner and Stevenson (1982) and Kessel and Siegel (1983).
2. UNICEF, *The State of the World's Children*. New York: Oxford University Press. Prepared by Peter Adamson and James P. Grant.

3. Bardy *et al* (1990) and Qvortrup (1993).
4. SCF-UK (1995).
5. Council of Europe (1995). See also the other reports on this issue by the same rapporteur and collaborators.
6. Bronfenbrenner (1979) and James and Prout (1990). See also, for example, Alston (1994).
7. Qvortrup (1993), pages 13ff.
8. Qvortrup (1993), pages 13ff.
9. See, among others, O'Neil (1985), (1988) and (1992), Freeman (1992) and Van Bueren (1995).
10. Geertz (1959).
11. Dahl (1993).
12. Were (1978).
13. My summary adapted from Were (1978).
14. There is increasing interest in the interdependency among the materialistic, technological and mental dimensions which Popper and Eccles call the 'three worlds'. See Popper and Eccles (1977).

    The International Development Research Centre of Canada (IDRC) has recently launched a research programme to examine the consequences for the dominant economic 'development paradigm' of spirituality, culture and economic development. See IDRC (1995).

    Chandra Muzaffar and others are advocating similar departures from non-Western philosophical and sociological traditions. See Muzaffar (1991).

    Paul Feyerabend and Georg von Wright, although representing very different philosophical views, have raised probing and provocative questions concerning the dominance of a scientific and technological 'regime of truth' and the hegemony of the 'technosystem'. See Feyerabend (1975) and (1978) and von Wright (1986), (1993) and (1994). See also Knutsson (1979) and (forthcoming).
15. Knutsson (1980).
16. Ryan (1995), pages 35ff.
17. Alston (1994), page 20.
18. Olsen (1992), page 195.
19. Caldwell (1983).
20. Caldwell (1983), page 7.
21. Caldwell (1983), page 9.
22. Caldwell (1983), page 11.
23. Knutsson (1970).
24. Blanchet (1996), page 38.

Essay 4: Different debates, different children

Despite some admittedly promising advances in conditions among children, many questions remain. If, as some might argue, there is a new willingness in rich and poor nations to take the needs and rights of children more seriously, why has this not resulted in action on a scale which would turn the incidence of hungry children, working children and street children into exceptional anecdotes instead of notable features of the situation in many countries? What makes the majority of those in power talk about children as 'our most precious asset' and at the same time support policies and permit processes which damage the physical and social environment of children? To be fair, survival rates among children are improving, but if, by 'survival', we mean survival in a life of fulfilment, then we need to admit that the century of the child that Ellen Key dreamt about one hundred years ago is still very far away.

Undoubtedly, the knowledge and ethical energy required to respond to our concerns exist, but they are not yet sufficiently integrated into the theories, policies and practices of what has thus far been mainly an economic approach to development. If the knowledge of problems and their causes exists but is not acted upon, then we must delve into the reasons why we cannot make the shift from knowing to doing.

On a planet increasingly influenced by the 'world view' of the proponents of science and technology, physical existence has come to be regarded as synonymous with 'reality' and 'existence'. We should understand, however, that physical existence alone and the possibility to measure and describe it are not sufficient either for a description of reality or for an understanding of it. We must distinguish between that which we can observe and document and that to which we can relate and add value and meaning and with which we can interact. Only that to which we actively assign purpose and meaning has significant existence. When we discuss the situation of children, it is obvious that the existence of the child and the conditions of its existence are totally dependent on what the child means to us. If the child is regarded as expendable, care will be inadequate and infant mortality rates and other indicators will be negative. In destitute villages, in the marginalized neighbourhoods of minorities and refuges, in the rapidly expanding environment of cities, especially the megacities, isolated, neglected, abandoned and exploited children are experiencing the consequences of this attitude. They are treated with abuse precisely because they are regarded as refuse.

The discrepancy between talk and action in relation to children is difficult to understand if we look at the size of the child population. In the poorer countries alone there are at least 1.8 billion children, easily the largest developing 'nation' in the world. Taken globally, the number swells to around 2 billion out of the 5.3 billion people presently crowding planet Earth. Especially in the poorer countries, children are the very symbol of what a concept of underdevelopment might signify, that is, the lack of control over one's own life.

The debates on children and childhood

There are at least three major debates on children and the efforts to better their situation. There is a theoretical debate which aims at analysing the problems of children, their causes and the linkages among them; there is a policy debate over the course of action to be taken to solve these problems; and there is an advocacy debate through which the cause of children is being argued and promoted.

The theoretical debate

One important type of theoretical contribution evident in the debate on betterment for children consists of research focusing on the psychomotor aspects of the child's biological and mental growth. This research has generated a special discipline revolving around what is called 'child development' and sometimes, because of its specific attention to the early phases of the child's life, as 'early child development'.

Until recently the term 'child development' was linked mainly to the physical, psychological and to some extent the social growth of the individual child. The theoretical debate has therefore been heavily concentrated within psychology, pædiatrics, early childhood care and education.

In recent decades a powerful theoretical influence has been exerted on child studies by the work of Piaget, who has come to dominate much of the public and professional discussion on child issues, as well as the practice of early childcare and education.[1] This work has relied on the assumption that 'child development has a particular structure, consisting of a series of predetermined stages which lead towards the eventual achievement of logical competence'.[2] The concept of competence as used here is based on a definition of adult rationality. The development of children is viewed as the process of the acquisition of increasing rationality through children's play and other activities as the children evolve through a predetermined sequence of steps towards maturity and the ultimate goal of adulthood. In this process children are perceived as beings queuing, as it were, in order to acquire the cognitive skills which will allow them to leave a 'primitive' state of existence (childhood) behind. Little importance is allotted to their individual lives in society or to differences in the environments in which they grow up.

The Piaget tradition has begun to be countered in recent studies by scholars who demand that children and childhood be accorded recognition and respect, theoretically and ethically, in their own right and on their own terms. However, in the meantime the dominant Piagetan concepts and interpretations have been extended beyond the theoretical discourse into the broader fields of professional opinion and practice in childcare and education. Criticisms of the assumptions and of the analysis in the Piagetan approach therefore meet with a wider resistance than they would have done if this had been a matter of theoretical controversy only. As James and Prout have pointed out:

> resistance to new (non-Piagetan) ways of thinking about childhood extends beyond the confines of sociology. There is a correspondence between the concepts of the social sciences and the ways in which childhood is socially constructed. Notions like socialization are inscribed in the practices of teachers and social workers.[3]

This recalls the 'regimes of truth' referred to by Foucault.[4] The way people, especially professionals dealing with children, think about childhood is blended together with institutional practices which build on the same premises, so that parents and teachers think and feel about children in the very same terms. Their perceptions take on the quality of truth in a mutually supporting interaction among outlooks and actions and the norms guiding both. To replace this with another 'truth' grounded in another way of thinking about childhood is as difficult as it is necessary.

Because it relies on a hierarchical series of value-based development stages from primitive to less primitive, the method of Piaget can be placed squarely within the evolutionist tradition. It exhibits the same general weaknesses in terms of the transfer to cultural analysis of biological models of explanation and the inclination to favour deductive and deterministic theories. Indeed, it is paradoxical that, while psychomotor-oriented child development studies have undoubtedly contributed to an improved understanding of important aspects of children and childhood, they have also strengthened certain false and detrimental notions which tend to view the child as isolated. They have therefore become a major obstacle to efforts aimed at opening a meaningful discourse on the location of children in society, on processes of betterment and on the issue of children's rights.

Scholars like Bronfenbrenner, Liljeström, Qvortrup, Cunningham, James and Prout, Jenks and others are proposing new theoretical underpinnings for an alternative perception of children and childhood which emphasizes the 'embeddedness' of the child in physical, social, cultural and political environments which require mapping and analysis.[5] Such an approach is necessary in order to connect the debate on the development *of* children with the discussion about development *for* children. However, the inertia impeding intellectual change and the time lag slowing the percolation of ideas among the communities of scholars and practitioners represent formidable barriers. Moreover, the perception of the child as isolated has an emotional appeal and strength which are very difficult to counter.

Another important, though generally much weaker, theoretical contribution evident in the debate on betterment for children centres on reflections about economic, social and political development for children. These reflections aim primarily at deepening our understanding of the situation in which children live, the structures and social processes affecting children and the nature of the strategies designed and applied so as to improve the conditions surrounding children. Although major linkages doubtless exist between the two streams of discussion, there is often a confusion between the two that has hampered rather than facilitated analysis and understanding.

Due to the strength of the child development tradition and despite efforts to redirect and enrich the discourse, the overwhelming majority of the theoretical literature which has emerged on the broader issues of development for children still falls into the category of studies of early childcare, health and education. However, the issues of gender equity, child labour and children in war and other especially difficult circumstances are increasingly claiming more attention. Nonetheless, apart from the information collected and disseminated by specific international children's agencies and non-government organizations, the situation of children and childhood has thus far generally been absent from economic and political theories about development of whatever type. In order to include children and childhood in the discourse on economic development and human betterment, new and serious theoretical efforts are needed within disciplines such as economics, political science and development theory.

The relative lack of child-specific data on the betterment of children and on overall development has been an important factor in the impoverishment of the theoretical debate on development for children as part of a process of economic and social development. Despite tremendous growth in the amount of development information, there is still a shortage in the fundamental child-specific data – including information about the views of children themselves – that is required for a better theoretical understanding of the situation of children and for policymaking and advocacy. The shortage is universal. This may seem surprising given that children make up more than one-third of the world's population. In any case, it is a revealing example of the effect of the widely held perception of children and childhood as quite inconsequential to 'serious' political and economic planning. This is especially harmful in the many poor countries where social statistics and other general data evaluations are not readily available. Some initiatives have been undertaken to rectify this problem, and improvements are noticeable, especially in relation to health statistics.[6] Nonetheless, the basic problem remains.

Indeed, industrialized and post-industrial societies face a similar problem. Children are generally invisible in statistics and in many other types of social, economic and political account-taking. A research group which is monitoring the situation of children in 19 European countries has pointed out that children are:

> not covered in available research, statistics, government reports, etc. In most cases they [are] virtually absent, while on the other hand [there was] information about adults who one way or another surrounded them.... The best which could be done was to make patchwork of bits of information, which, in most cases, [were] not collected with the purpose of telling about children, but in which children were somehow involved. Children were split up into categories that were not really relevant for [the] understanding of their life conditions....[7]

The policy debate

In many developing countries and especially in rural areas, traditional processes for the integration of children still prevail, although all too often social integration takes the form of exploitation and excessive work, especially for girls, both inside and outside the home. In countries where material resources are not major limitations, children tend to be marginalized in other ways. They are often without meaningful contacts with the workplace and other major environments of adult life. Many spend a major part of their time in schools and daycare centres or with their peers. Like the elderly, they are in many instances considered a nuisance by the so-called productive age groups. People sometimes mask their anti-child attitudes by showering children with an abundance of material goods so as to compensate for the guilt they feel because of the neglect they practise.

There is, however, an increasing recognition, at least rhetorically, that children and their needs are legitimate political concerns. To a great extent this has been achieved because of intense advocacy over a long period by numerous non-government organizations and by UNICEF. These efforts received an important boost in the years leading up to and immediately following the International Year of the Child (1979). They have also been aided by the progress registered through some large-scale programmes for children.

The World Summit for Children, an important meeting of heads of state and senior cabinet members from 150 countries in 1990, adopted very specific and time-bound goals for children and promised to produce national plans of action to reach these goals.

The Convention on the Rights of the Child states that all children have certain fundamental rights regardless of culture, creed, colour or level of income. This 'Bill of Rights', which has thus far been ratified by 190 countries, amounts to a veritable constitution of the 'nation' of children, and the work to achieve these rights is beginning to receive more attention.

The central issues in the policy debate concerning children revolve around the factors which influence the political will in favour of children, child rights, the nature of the citizenship which ought to be accorded to children and the participation of children.

Political will

The perceptions of children and childhood associated with policy differ depending on the level and the local environment of the policymakers. As a comparison between child-related policies in Scandinavia and those in the US or between child-related policies in Sri Lanka and those in Pakistan would vividly illustrate, positive child policies are essentially a matter of political choice. However, such policies are also influenced by public demands and by cost calculations. Children may be lauded as assets or as citizens of the future, but policymakers may actually be more concerned about children as expenditure items in national accounts. In fact, the existence of political will as a precondition in efforts to improve the situation of children is to a great extent dependent on cost concerns. If the cost is low, the political will can be high. On the other hand, if the projected expenditures seem high, although they may be low in comparison to other investments deemed more prestigious, the willingness to make political choices for the betterment of children tends to decrease steeply.

Because of this relationship between costs and political feasibility, much of the international debate on children since the 1980s has been devoted to the matter of costs, and a major part of the progress which has been achieved in some large-scale programmes, especially in preventive primary health care, has been due to the availability of and the advocacy for low-cost measures. However, the preference for such measures is in itself an indication of a low level of political interest in children – and therefore of political will for children – relative to other political goals.

Child rights

The major portion of the policy debate on children which has centred on children's rights has mostly focused on the legal interpretation of the various articles of the Convention on the Rights of the Child.[8] However, it has also involved wide-ranging discussions on development goals for children and on the resources, public and otherwise, that would be required to institute the various children's rights, as well as discussions in national, regional and international forums on programmes and on strategic issues.[9] Furthermore, the adoption of the Convention has stimulated a great deal of fresh awareness about some of the most heinous violations of children's rights, such as abusive child labour, discrimination against girls, the commercial sexual exploitation of children, children in war, and minority children and discrimination.

Some of the issues in these discussions deserve to be raised more openly. One of these issues relates to certain of the philosophical and legal concerns about the specific nature of rights and obligations in regard to children. Another relates to the rather widespread perception in many non-Western countries that there is a considerable cultural bias in certain aspects of children's rights. If these particular issues are not examined more seriously, there is a risk that the criticism of the child rights movement will not be effectively countered.

Two of the most eloquent opponents or, at least, naysayers of children's rights are Onora O'Neill and Laura Purdy.[10] Purdy asks the question: should children have equal rights? She summarizes the possible answers in the following way.

> At present different rights are recognized for adults and children. Some adults' rights free them to act in accordance with their own judgment; they are considered competent to make a wide variety of decisions ranging from what to wear to whom to marry. Children, on the contrary, are denied these rights on the ground that children are irrational. Their alleged irrationality justifies protecting them in ways that also limit their freedom.
>
> Proponents of equal rights contend, however, that in reality children are no more irrational than the least competent adult. Hence, there is no morally relevant difference between the two classes, and the divergent laws that apply to children constitute unjust discrimination, discrimination that oppresses children.[11]

Although Purdy shows a certain amount of sympathy for a more liberal approach towards child rights, she actually sides quite strongly with a much more restrictive approach which, she argues, will in the end be more protective of children because it will give greater weight to the punishment of harmful acts than to the restriction of freedom. In her view an approach which balances children's rights and the rights of adults would severely hamper children's opportunities to evolve skills and acquire abilities for a constructive adulthood. It could even undermine education and propel children into the workplace.

O'Neill voices similar views. She argues that if we care about children's lives, 'There are good reasons not to base our arguments on appeals to children's fundamental rights ... their fundamental remedy is to grow up.'[12]

Those who propose that children's rights be approached as much as possible in ways similar to the approach taken towards human rights in general argue against both these outlooks. Michael Freeman summarizes this position.

> It cannot be right, as O'Neill states, that the child's 'main remedy is to grow up'. First, she underestimates the capacities and maturity of many children. Both in moral and [in] cognitive development, many children reach adult levels between 12 and 14.... We expect adolescents to be criminally responsible at the age of 14 (indeed, we are prepared to impose criminal responsibility on them at 10), but we are less willing to accept the correlativity of responsibility and rights.... There are very few (if any) absolute rights, and these must by definition belong to children, too.[13]

The disagreements are certainly much more complicated and nuanced than this brief summary suggests. However, it is very clear that all those who are working for the betterment of children ought to become aware of the rights formulated in the Convention and the reasoning behind them so that they can more effectively promote these rights.

There also exist fundamental concerns about a perceived cultural bias in the concepts both of human rights and of child rights. These concerns tend to focus on a valuation, supposedly specific to Western and industrialized societies, that the independence of the individual is basic to all human rights and therefore also to child rights. In this view, for example, the child's right to belong to a society and to participate in a culture may be sacrificed because of a preference in the recognition of rights to freedom and independence. In other words, there is a bias in favour of individual achievement over social cohesion and cultural congeniality. There is a concern in many societies that the proponents of universal children's rights are supporting culturally biased goals, such as the right to individual experimentation, over the right to proper guidance. Unfortunately, this genuine concern is often used to justify customs which are in flagrant violation of any moral standard, let alone a universalist one.

There is no easy solution to this controversy. There may even be no solution whatsoever. Nonetheless, the best hope for achieving a long-lasting agreement on the nature of children's rights and on reasonable and effective ways to protect these rights lies in a thorough awareness of the various views.

Childhood and citizenship

A major factor behind the invisibility of children in politics and policy-making is the fact that children are not recognized as full and worthy members of society. In being excluded from the enjoyment of political rights, children are in the company of lunatics and criminals.[14] In the classical world in the West, only free men, especially those with means or who were not menial labourers, were considered full citizens. During the French Revolution, women, the mentally ill and minors did not have full rights, while the American Constitution excluded women and slaves.

Indirectly, through its various articles on the survival, protection and development of the child and the articles dealing with the right of the child to individual and collective identity, the Convention on the Rights of the Child extends many of the rights of citizenship to the child. However, if the problem of invisibility is to be effectively tackled, the issue of the full and worthy membership of the child in society has to be dealt with directly and unambiguously.

In an important programmatic statement for the study *Children as a Social Phenomenon*, Qvortrup poses the question of whether society should bear any responsibility for children. He proceeds by identifying three basic arguments for assuming that it should.

First, he claims that there is 'a moral argument for ensuring that children are provided for in accordance with a basic standard, or a standard for a family with children which is in line with that of couples without children'.[15] This sort of argument is often heard in industrial societies. It may be generalized thus: the technological, social, economic, political and knowledge standards required for a family to attain basic security in all these dimensions should not penalize the family in relation to other members of society by the circumstance that the family has additional responsibilities for children.

Second, Qvortrup offers the 'achievement' argument which is based on the fact that children contribute to the reproduction of society biologically, organizationally and culturally. Children thus have a legitimate claim to share in all the various dimensions of social and cultural life. One might also agree with the author 'that it would not be unwarranted' for parents to have a similar claim on additional resources for their share in this contribution. Taken a step further, this becomes an argument which, in the words of Qvortrup, 'relates "interest" in children with responsibility for children, and it is not difficult to demonstrate that society also has a number of interests in children, if not in children while they are children, then at least in … what is called the next generation'.[16] Society ought to take an interest in children while they are children not merely for emotional reasons or because of a sense of charity, but for practical reasons. After all, children are the co-creators of the present and the builders of the future.

Third is the 'utilitarian' argument for the inclusion of concerns for children and childhood in serious social, economic and political considerations. According to this argument, the participation of children in the education system and other institutions and organizations designed to prepare them eventually to bear responsibility for the continued existence of society and culture represents a form of labour. This should be interpreted as a plea for the recognition of, for instance, school labour, which cannot justifiably be separated from other forms of labour in society at large, particularly since it is integrally interwoven with the needs of the larger labour market.[17]

Children, participation and the right to be heard

Participation is a basic value in democratic governance.[18] This does not mean that participation and the conditions under which one is eligible to participate are uniform or coherent. Nonetheless, despite the variations, the discussion on children's participation revolves around two major deficiencies which participation strategies need to address. One relates to the institutionalized restrictions within the social and cultural space for children. Participatory approaches aim to expand this space and at the same time raise the social and cultural competence of the child. The other major deficiency relates to the distortions and ruptures which have occurred in relationships, especially in industrialized societies, because of the rapidly expanding sectoralization and compartmentalization within social life. The effects of these distortions and ruptures are visible, for example, in education systems. As De Winter points out:

> As the worlds of children and adults were pulled further apart, a process that ... had already started in the fifteenth century, the direct presentation of adult ways of life to children was increasingly impeded. Because children were less directly involved in the day-to-day reality of their parents and the community, the possibilities for them to familiarize themselves with its content and structure through experience fell away. Instead of this, the educational genre of representation developed. Education was no longer a confrontation with reality, but a reflection of reality.[19]

The debate on children's participation is still vague.[20] In order to sharpen it, we need to distinguish between active and passive participation, among political, social and economic participation and between the participation of children with other children for their own purposes and the participation of children with adults in areas of common concern. The levels at which participation occurs or ought to occur represent another important distinction.

The opposition to children's participation has strong roots, and the arguments raised against participation are widely endorsed. In a recent and incisive overview Lansdown has pointed out the following:

The view that children have a right to participate in decisions affecting their lives provokes a number of responses from families in all cultures....

- children are not competent to participate in decision-making
- giving children rights threatens the harmony and stability of family life
- children cannot have rights until they are able to exercise responsibilities
- imposing responsibilities detracts from the right to childhood.[21]

Other arguments against children's participation are often put forward. One argument is based on the fact that childhood is transient and constantly depleted of its strongest and most competent members as adolescents enter into adult life. Within childhood itself there are not only significant biological and social discrepancies among separate age groups, but also dramatic variations in culture, status and resources depending on differences in the upbringing of children and in the communities to which they belong. The participation of children in movements similar to the women's movement or to the movements of minorities for civil rights is therefore difficult to envisage.[22]

However, these sorts of obstacles need not be viewed as reasons for defeatism, but could serve as inspiration for the development of new approaches and strategies. The few successful attempts which have been tried speak volumes about the opportunities. There have been sound efforts to establish movements by groups of children against bonded labour in many countries in South Asia.[23] A movement among street children in Brazil eventually managed to mobilize public opinion and supportive politicians and secure access both to the Parliament and to the head of state so that the children could present their grievances, as well as their own constructive proposals for action, and at the same time build national support for the Convention on the Rights of the Child.[24]

In a film from Gujarat, India, Maj Wechselman has documented a movement by children for children. The teenage daughters of some of the wealthy landowners decided to feed and care for the children of thousands of bonded labourers from the Kojta tribal group who every year are herded together in the neighbouring state of Maharashtra and forced to walk hundreds of kilometres to the fields of the sugar lords in Gujarat. The daughters of the landowners could not stand the suffering which they witnessed and so they began their movement for the protection and survival of the bonded children. They were threatened with rape and murder. The makeshift shelters which they had built with their own hands to serve as childcare centres were torn down. Nonetheless, they persisted and they finally found support for their child-to-child initiative.

This is true development based on children's immediate experience of sorrow and responsibility, founded on a fellowship of pain and translated into the practice of love and solidarity despite threats and violence. Are situations of war and civil strife and the struggles on the streets of slums and unauthorized squatter settlements so different?

It is tempting to speculate about the effects of such efforts if they were to be tried on a larger scale. Would it not be possible for better-off children to live for a while in urban slums in order to learn about the real conditions of their fellow child citizens? What if the children of the slums, together with their friends from the postcard neighbourhoods, were to join up and speak together in great numbers about their two separate city environments? Could not children be encouraged to talk about their experiences as child labourers, child prostitutes and children in war? If given a chance, children could serve as bridges to peace and messengers of solidarity. If nations and communities which ignore the right of children to be protected from abject poverty, armed conflict and structural violence, especially against girls and women, can be stimulated or shamed into action, then there might also be hope for conflict resolution on a larger scale.

In an important contribution to the debate on children's participation, Roger Hart has used a healthy combination of pragmatism and commitment to argue for the right of children to be heard. He stresses the importance of adult involvement in participatory efforts for the counsel which they can offer, but also for the lessons which they need to learn. Building on Arnstein's work, he sharpens the definition of the concept of participation by excluding tactics of manipulation, 'decoration' and tokenism. He distinguishes between the weaker forms of participation, such as the assignation of rather passive (token) roles or mere consultation and information sharing, and activities in which children participate in decisions and initiatives or in which they have some 'management' control.[25] He remains sceptical of 'easy' forms of large-scale mobilization, but comes out strongly in favour of genuine participation, including participation in partnership with adults. He especially underlines the importance of children's participation so that they can understand their own situations, especially when these are difficult. He also argues that the benefits of participation are dramatic for the development of social skills, responsibility in community development and political self-determination.[26]

The advocacy debate

This involves important components contained in the other major aspects of the overall debate on development for children. However, the overriding preoccupation is with analysis, theory, policy and action. Thus far, the major share of the discussion on children in development has taken place within the advocacy debate. One type of approach is ethical and based on what is considered morally imperative. This approach is generally presented as universally valid, although the arguments may actually rely on culture-specific values which are relevant to the groups promoting the arguments and which are not shared by groups outside the centres of advocacy. The discussion on child labour offers many examples of this sort of argument.

The exploitation of children in any situation is clearly unacceptable. However, it must not be confused with more normal situations where children are encouraged to participate in adult work through minor contributions. Such participation provides opportunities for learning and offers important feedback in terms of recognition of children's contributions, respect and a sense of achievement. In the best of situations, play and work-like contributions, rights and obligations can be combined. Admittedly, the borderlines among these roles are difficult to draw and easy to cross. The joy of a six-year-old looking after the family sheep during the morning hours in the vicinity of his home in the Ethiopian highlands can turn into pain in the hot midday sun. An eight-year-old girl in the Chittagong Hill tracts may be pleased to take her younger brother on her hip for a while, but will be suffering physically and mentally if she is obliged to turn this playful encounter into a day-long duty.

Facts and figures are used in the advocacy debate to illustrate both the ethical imperatives behind goals and the feasibility of achieving these goals. Whenever possible, the justification for accepting the advocacy proposals has been grounded on economic, political and sociological knowledge. The political appetite is whetted by references to attractive cost-benefit ratios and to enlightened self-interest both in the shorter and longer term perspective. Kerala's and Sri Lanka's earlier combinations of egalitarian economic policies, supportive social measures, universal education and accompanying low birth and infant mortality rates have become standard examples in this context. Other arguments link the need to address the problems confronting children with already widespread concerns about the environment and gender discrimination.

The advocacy debate on children is greatly conditioned by the location of the observer or advocate and the perspectives from which adult society and its organizations choose to see children and childhood. Because of this, there is an urgent need to look not only at how various organizations perceive children, but also at how they look upon themselves and their roles. We know very little about these fundamental cultural aspects of UNICEF and other international organizations, for instance, or about similar characteristics among governments and non-government organizations. However, such knowledge is essential for effective communication as well as for efforts to promote a fruitful division of labour in programmes or areas requiring joint action. What we do know is that the nature of the assumptions and perceptions which the members of an organization hold about themselves and their mission will decisively influence their advocacy position, their policy approach, their goals, the content of their work and their presentation of this content.

Where precise policy and its articulation in advocacy are lacking, or where they are not clearly understood or digested, other underlying assumptions – borrowed or inherited – will automatically take their place and determine attitudes and influence action.

'Positional' perspectives

Depending on the position and location of observers, perceptions and views will vary significantly – including among those people who work for the betterment of children. In certain cases positional perspectives have led to a great deal of misunderstanding. An illustration of the need to be aware of these perspectives is found in Liljeström's distinction between 'the private child', 'the commercial child' and the 'public child'.[27] However, such variations and perspectives are rarely identified, recognized or discussed and are therefore forced, as it were, underground, generating frustrations, organizational frictions and other negative outcomes.

For example, there exist within UNICEF, and probably within other child development organizations as well, rather 'dialectic' positional attitudes which have had a great influence on the perceptions about children and the nature of the debate on children. Thus, as Jonsson has pointed out, there are two distinct sets of preferences within the organization: one focused on achieving a certain objective or outcome, sometimes at the expense of other needs, and the other emphasizing the importance of the choice of an approach or a process which will help strengthen participation, solidify and sustain achievements and foster capacities for the future.[28] These two sets of preferences are not confined to any specific location or level of work; they can be found among many different groups of staff. However, in practice, the first position tends to be centred on headquarters and on a policy-oriented perspective, and the second is more frequently found in the 'field', where there is a stronger relationship with programme realities. Major problems arise because these differences are neither articulated nor understood, and the debate which they generate is therefore often very emotional. The high level of emotion may also be partly due to the differences in 'power' among the proponents of the two perspectives.

The responsibility at the policy level for political and financial support, as well as for far-reaching communication for the mobilization of public opinion, has a decisive influence on attitudes in a headquarters environment. Similarly, a field position, with its closeness to human and local political realities and to the practical problems in implementing policies, is subject to corresponding conditioning effects.

Perceived from a policy standpoint, the child tends to be the important unit of attention. The focus on the child favours concrete presentations and facilitates comparisons among countries based on specific indicators. The focus is on goals, especially on the more concrete, short-term ones. Strategies for reaching children tend to be technology- and efficiency-oriented. The inclination is to emphasize opportunities. The communication of messages and the interpretation of trends are usually optimistic, since fundraising and mobilization need to be fuelled.

From a field position, a rather different set of preferences becomes visible. Children in their many and varied environments are the major focus of attention. Goals are generally viewed in a broad sense and more long term. Strategies tend to be system oriented and to recognize the complexities of governments and communities, the problems facing them, the multiple nature of causative factors and the impediments to change that they generate. Opportunities are welcomed, but the awareness of problems and obstacles is strong. There is an atmosphere of cautiousness since results need to be sustained over time for both ethical and economic reasons and also in order to preserve the credibility of the organization and the rationale for its presence.

The effects on perceptions and strategy choices are similar in other contexts and on many other levels. For example, a medical doctor in a village setting may strongly recommend investment in child health as the overriding priority. A local farmer may agree with this theoretical assessment. However, because the farmer is responsible for the long-term viability of an entire household and its members, he may well choose the purchase of an ox as his policy priority. A dialogue which would favour a reasonable compromise between the two 'positional' perspectives and over time lead to greater attention to health concerns may be missed because the farmer's policy and programme priority are misinterpreted as ignorance about health needs or as lack of compassion for his children. Instead, the difficult choices facing the farmer should be more clearly understood and respected. Only then can a fruitful effort at advocacy be initiated which will also benefit other members of the farmer's household, including the children.

Such differences in perspective are not peculiar to work for the betterment of the lives of children nor to development cooperation in general. They can be found at various levels in many other organizations, public or private, which are regional or global in nature. The best way to avoid misinterpreting any perspective is not to put it automatically into a simplistic list of right or wrong depending on one's own position, but to become aware of it and of the reasoning behind it and to deal with the differences openly. For example, the two major sets of perspectives within UNICEF are often wrongly categorized as a more theoretical and a more practical preference. Instead, the two perspectives should be seen as poles in one and the same spectrum of tasks. Such a view would have important consequences in problem identification and in the formulation of working strategies which would enhance 'complementarities' and partnerships. It should be seriously considered in the assessment of qualifications in staff and in training programmes.

The preliminary divisions of the debate on children into separate theoretical, policy and advocacy debates is an important one. It helps us to realize that in the theoretical debate the 'child' is to a great extent a construction of psychological observation, pædiatric care and educational concern, whereas the perceptions and valuations of the child from the position of policymakers are coloured by concerns specific to policy. To many politicians the dominant perception is that of a 'costly child' rather than of a valuable citizen. There is also an 'advocacy child', or, if one takes a somewhat more cynical view, a 'fundraising child' who has been created and promoted in order to foster among potential contributors a sense that there is an emotional and moral attachment and therefore a personal obligation to provide support and resources for children in need. Such motives are behind the thousands of touching pictures we see of children with wasted bodies and aged faces covered with flies.

Notes and references

1. Burman (1994).
2. James and Prout (1990), page 11.
3. James and Prout (1990), page 23.
4. Foucault (1977).
5. Bronfenbrenner (1979), Liljeström (1983), Qvortrup (1993), Cunningham (1995), James and Prout (1990) and Jenks (1996).
6. Work in this direction was undertaken by the UNICEF Regional Office for Eastern and Southern Africa in the 1980s and by the UNICEF Regional Office for South Asia in the early 1990s.
7. Qvortrup *et al* (1994), pages 6ff. See also SCF-UK (1995), pages 33ff.
8. See Alston, Parker and Seymour (1992) and Alston (1994).
9. See UNICEF (1990) and Himes (1995). As a follow-up to the adoption of the Convention on the Rights of the Child and to the World Summit for Children, a series of high-level regional meetings was convened in the early 1990s which produced regional endorsements and statements of goals. An example is the Colombo Summit of the countries of the South Asia Association for Regional Cooperation which was held in Colombo, Sri Lanka, in 1991 and which was preceded by extensive regional consultations on major issues linked to the Convention and the Summit. See Matthai (1992).
10. O'Neill (1985) and (1988) and Purdy (1992).
11. Purdy (1992), page 211.
12. O'Neill (1992), page 39.
13. Freeman (1992), pages 58ff.
14. See De Winter (1995), page 15.
15. Qvortrup (1993), page 17.
16. Qvortrup (1993), page 17.

17. Qvortrup (1993), page 14.
18. UNDP (1993). For a comprehensive discussion of the issue of participation in all its many aspects, see Stiefel and Wolfe (1994).
19. De Winter (1995), page 40.
20. See, for example, West (1996).
21. Lansdown (1995), page 20.
22. For example, see O'Neill (1992).
23. See Freeman (1992).
24. Hart (1992), pages 31ff.
25. Arnstein (1979) and Hart (1992), pages 8ff.
26. For an extensive discussion of these issues in concrete settings in Africa, Asia, Latin America and Europe, see Taylor *et al* (1995).
27. See Liljeström (1983).
28. Jonsson (1996).

Essay 5: The debate in practice: the case of UNICEF

For our inquiry into the nature of the international debate on children and childhood and the betterment of their condition, we also need to consider the debate 'in practice' as reflected in actual policies and programmes for children. Because of the nature of the author's own exposure, this analysis will be restricted mainly to the experience within the United Nations and especially to the work of UNICEF.

Maggie Black has described the various stages of UNICEF's practice and some of the assumptions underlying it in her broad and penetrating overview in *The Children and the Nations*.[1] The discussion here is greatly indebted to her excellent analysis of an institutional history within the larger framework of human betterment.

In the international concern for children and the efforts to better their situation, the establishment of the Save the Children movement in the 1920s represents a milestone. From this seed, a rich flora of voluntary and non-government organizations has grown. Already existing entities, such as the network of the Red Cross and Red Crescent associations, were stimulated to orient much of their work towards children in need. Within the United Nations, UNICEF was created much later, after the Second World War, as an expression of the commitment of nations to this same cause. In addition, the specialized agencies of the United Nations were given broad mandates for their work, which included initiatives aimed at children and young people.

Beside the leadership of strong and sensitive people, many factors were behind this expanded concern for children. These were preceded by a public debate stretching over more than a century. This debate grew out of the struggle against slavery and the ensuing concern for working and abandoned children. Shifts in the moral climate were triggered by the First World War, the humanitarian catastrophes in Russia and recurrent famines, especially in Southern and Eastern Asia. The horrors of the Second World

War and the problems in its wake in Europe and in Asia were brought to the public eye by increasingly effective media coverage.

Out of the rising public awareness emerged an 'emergency-humanitarian approach' to the alleviation of child suffering. The principle goal of this approach was to save children's lives and to protect children from disease and want. The emergency-humanitarian cluster was dominated by the perception of the child as isolated and it focused on direct charitable interventions. Because of the circumstances typical of an emergency, this was generally unavoidable. Starving children need to be provided immediately with food, water, medical assistance and shelter.

UNICEF, which was established in 1946 as a temporary organization to continue the work for children of the United Nations Relief and Rehabilitation Agency in the chaotic and traumatic aftermath of the Second World War, was dedicated during its first years to responding to emergencies in Central Europe and in the war-ravaged countries of East Asia. In 1953, it was given a permanent and global mandate to assist children in poor countries. Much of UNICEF's work during this first decade of its existence was concentrated on the need to protect children from hunger and disease. Supplementary feeding schemes were supported, and threats to health such as tuberculosis, yaws and malaria were vigorously fought through intensive campaigns.

Development: concern for the whole child

A development approach – albeit one with a limited ambition based on the prevalent ideology of economic growth – eventually began to influence the thinking on betterment for children. Among the most prominent rationales for this approach was the idea that children ought to be allowed to grow to their full potential both physically and intellectually. While this was in some ways similar to the human rights approach, it was mainly based on the idea that, through such growth, the child will eventually become a more mature, useful and 'effective' citizen as an adult. Research and experience indicated that there were strong correlations between, on the one hand, proper care and education for children and, on the other, overall economic growth, which was the main goal of the ideology and practice of developmentalism at the time.

The strategies and programmes of the development approach emphasized the strengthening of the systems, services, personnel and competencies upon which the welfare of children depends. This represented an important, although rarely highlighted, step away from the perception of the isolated child towards a more integrated view of children and childhood.

In the 1950s, UNICEF undertook decentralization and enhanced its field representation. The nature of the real problems facing children became recognized more readily through the close linkages fostered by UNICEF's leadership between field experience and policy considerations.

Meanwhile, new ideas emerged in the international debate. Some of these were based on the realization that the effectiveness of the emergency approach was limited.

> The most powerful of the new ideas was the perception of people's needs as interlocking parts of a puzzle, necessarily to be met only by interlocking responses. The theory of community development was that a multipronged programme with complementary ingredients could tackle the poverty problem of an entire community. By the same token, the interlocking problems affecting children could only be addressed by a mix of complementary ingredients, and, as children were not a socially separate group, but intimately dependent on their families and the wider community, interlocking programmes for children must also interlock with those for other family members and the community at large.[2]

During the 1950s and early 1960s, the community development approach represented the first major attempt to break out of the isolated child syndrome. It took many of its theoretical and strategic cues from functionalist anthropological and sociological community analyses, especially in Latin America, India and the US. However, in practice it soon became distorted by attempts to implement the functionalist credo that everything depends on everything else. In addition, the emphasis on comprehensiveness in process and the tendency in the same intellectual tradition to value stability and coherence often made it difficult to deal with the problems of variations and change and to achieve a balance between a holistic understanding of problems and the need to be pragmatic and selective in action. Analytically and programmatically, the community development approach became dominated by outsiders, both internal and external, and this, together with the probably unintended creation of isolated islands of development with little or no prospect of replication, soon stymied efforts and reduced the initial enthusiasm.

The failure of internationally promoted community development was due largely to well-intentioned efforts to do things for the community rather than to create realistic political and economic opportunities and supportive partnerships among local communities, voluntary movements, professional expertise and government in order to enable communities to become meaningfully engaged.[3]

In this respect, the community development approach differed dramatically from the less theoretical and much more far-reaching mobilization of local communities for social development that was being undertaken by social reformers, political groups and grassroots movements. Some of the early religious and utopian movements in the US and the people's crusade for social causes in Scandinavia implemented more practical and successful concepts of community development. In the 1920s and 1930s the Gandhian movement achieved wide success in India, especially in terms of social mobilization, the generation of political awareness and an indigenous human rights crusade against the suppression characteristic of the colonial system and the oppression practised in the name of the caste system.

The experiences and traditions inspired by these and other efforts continue today especially in the work of non-government organizations, but also in so-called 'area programmes' which are supported by governments, donor countries and organizations such as UNICEF. The basic tenet behind the early community development initiatives that no betterment will be possible without the involvement of the communities which together make up the nation is still valid but rarely recognized by governments.

The conviction that there was an urgent need to consider the 'whole' child in the context of the development of the community started to gain momentum around the same time. Efforts were made to link the provision of supplies and training and to combine technical and logistical expertise. For example, it was recognized that the promotion of good weaning practices must interlock with disease control and both must become integrated within mother and child health care services. In September 1958, it was suggested for the first time to the UNICEF executive board that UNICEF should promote the intellectual, as well as the physical, well-being of the child.

In parallel with the orientation towards communities, large-scale undertakings were also designed and initiated. The dominant approach still involved campaign-like, geographically restricted efforts to reduce specific threats to the health of children. Among the most prominent initiatives were projects for the delivery and use of nutritional supplements and the provision of supplementary feeding products especially conceived for infants. These sorts of projects received a significant boost because of a rapidly growing concern with the damaging effects of protein malnutrition following the discovery by Cicely Williams of kwashiorkor, a specific form of severe protein deficiency, and the work of Newin Scrimshaw in Guatemala and of others in Africa and Asia on nutritional requirements.

To create a basis for its own policies, UNICEF decided to undertake a major survey of the needs of children. It argued that children should no longer be the 'orphans' of the development process.

> ...they should be a target of all policies and programmes directed at building up a country's human capital. The report prepared in the mid-1960s interwove all the relevant social and economic strands concerning children's well-being in a way which had never been done before. A theory of development was presented in which the satisfaction of children's needs during the various phases of childhood and pre-adulthood mattered deeply.[4]

This represented a breakthrough in development thinking that was far ahead of its time and that is still in need of advocacy and support 30 years after its conception.

Development planning and basic services

During the 1960s, UNICEF strengthened its advocacy in support of the conviction that children and their needs were central to mainstream development. High-level staff intensified their participation in discussions on development planning. Implicitly referring to the limitations of the charity and emergency approaches, they argued that 'there were reasons far more cogent than sentiment or humanitarian concern for taking children's needs into account in the national scheme of things'.[5]

At the beginning of the 1960s, the First Development Decade, planning was regarded principally as a tool for economic rather than social development. Where and when planning was applied to matters of human concern, it was mainly because human resources were regarded as an important aspect of and a condition for productive capital investment. Education, health care and other social services which focused on the development and maintenance of human capital were deemed necessary from an economic point of view. To provide these critical services, mobilization and training were needed.

However, in the mid-1960s the close linkage between the social and the economic aspects of the problems of poverty and underdevelopment began to be much more widely recognized. UNICEF's development philosophy that children – and people in general – mattered not only as tools for economic growth but also in their own right was in keeping with this evolution in thinking. The utilitarian argument was also put forward in order to promote the creation of the human resources necessary for economic growth and the development required to respond to people's needs as human beings and as family and community members. These views, which were increasingly discussed in concerned academic circles, were adopted by the International Labour Organization and provided the theoretical and political foundation for its 'basic needs' strategy. This strategy was soon being criticized in many developing countries because it seemed to be a prescription for a minimalist approach by the richer countries toward the problems of poor nations. However, during the late 1960s and early 1970s it provided inspiration for UNICEF's 'basic services' strategy.

In this context, UNICEF's suggestion that planning had as much to do with children as it did with irrigation works and public highways began to make more sense.[6] This outlook was soon reflected within UNICEF by the concept of integrated services for the whole child. To reach villagers, basic services had to be conceived, promoted and delivered as an integrated package. All the various sectors and environments affecting the child were represented in this strategy: health care and nutrition, education, water supply, sanitation, food conservation, family planning and support for women's activities. Instead of putting the emphasis on enhancing coordination among administrative departments at levels above the village, the new strategy aimed at making services come together in a mutually supportive way directly within communities.

The basic services concept was a major improvement in terms of social analysis, but also ethically because of its focus on the responsibility of the state and adult society to offer relevant and adequate services to children. It pointed forward to the emphasis on primary health care, which was an important step away from individually oriented treatment and towards the creation of a supportive and healthy society for the greatest possible number of citizens. Conceptually the basic services approach was on the right track, building as it did on a clear understanding of the need to abandon the concept of the isolated child in favour of the view that the child is embedded in the many layers of the social and cultural environment.

Despite its advantages, the strategy encountered major difficulties. One set of problems had its roots in the sectoralization of government structures, centralization and the lack of skills and resources for investment in service-supporting infrastructures. Another set of obstacles emanated from the shortage of experience in involving people and communicating with them as knowledgeable colleagues in development; this tended to encourage over-reliance on administrative solutions and service personnel, albeit on a much more realistic level and based on efforts which were more pragmatic than had been those characteristic of the charity or emergency approaches. Further complications arose because of the tendency to be so holistic in service delivery that initiatives often collapsed into the same small-scale and limited pilot and demonstration exercises which had been typical of the community development movement and which the strategy was explicitly meant to avoid.

Primary health care

As the recognition mounted of the social embeddedness of children's problems and therefore of the need to work in all of the environments of the child, UNICEF started to emphasize the overriding importance of improving child health. Standard health care procedures which were highly technical, costly and largely ineffective were coming under scrutiny, and the leaders of the World Health Organization and UNICEF realized that medicine had become 'a colossal industry with powerful vested interests, and that these interests dictated health policies unwisely and with punishing discrimination against the poor'.[7]

In keeping with this fundamental analysis, new directions were identified; these were endorsed at the Alma Ata Conference in 1978 which was jointly sponsored by WHO and UNICEF. The promotion and protection of the health of the people were considered essential in the attempt to sustain economic and social development and contribute to a better quality of life and eventually to world peace. The cornerstone of the new approach was the involvement of all major sectors and the recognition that people have the right and duty to participate individually and collectively in the planning and implementation of their own health care.

Within a few years the primary health care strategy had become significant among the efforts at health care promotion. Its principles, particularly that of community participation, represented a fresh ideology for health care. For nearly two decades, development had been delivered to the people. The people had not thought a great deal of it; it had rarely taken their views, beliefs and realities into serious account. Now the debate began finally to move in their direction. Advocated by pioneering groups of health care professionals and voluntary organizations, health by the people became the alternative theory in health care promotion.[8] The role of professionals and government services was to provide training, supervision, logistical support, material aid and technical advice. These concepts, echoing the spirit of the times and borrowing revolutionary fervour from the ideas of Paolo Freire on 'conscientization' and 'deschooling', 'gained excitement and appeal from their very antagonism to the existing structure of the medical world'.[9]

Child survival and development

The process of translating the principles of primary health care into practice and making a significant difference for a great number of people turned out to be disappointingly slow. In response to the gloomy prospects of implementing large-scale basic services and comprehensive primary health care at the same time, UNICEF decided in 1980 to raise with renewed energy the question of how to translate existing knowledge and experience into far-reaching action and mobilize the political and financial resources which such an expansion would require.[10]

There were many reasons for the poor outcomes of the lofty commitments taken at the Alma Ata Conference, where the world's governments had unanimously endorsed the new methods. Some had to do with the stubborn and competitive sectoralization of governments. Others revolved around the vested interests of professional and administrative cadres or quite frequently the absence of such cadres. Financial difficulties, the low political priority of child-related development and the distorted aims of the ideology of economic development were other factors which seemed to render the prospects slim.

Nonetheless, several politically and financially feasible initiatives with potentially significant impacts began to attract attention. Thus, the child survival and development strategy merged the development approach with the appeal of the emergency-humanitarian approach by expanding the emergency concept to cover disastrous eruptions of human misery and acute deprivation in so-called 'loud' emergencies, as well as the ongoing 'silent' emergencies which were crippling the lives of hundreds of millions of children through poverty, disease and hazardous and often abusive environments. The strategy also emphasized the need for a cost-effectiveness calculation to identify 'do-able' goals which could be promoted despite severe financial constraints.

'Survival' became the focus of activities which were supported by new technologies, including new communication technologies, and which were intended to reach a larger number of children and boost public awareness of the plight of children, thereby augmenting the resources available for children. To this, the concept of development was added. To start with, the stress was mainly on the optimum physical development of the child. Later, especially toward the end of the 1980s, primary education and child rights began to emerge as important complementary priorities.

The child survival and development strategy was based on the realization that visible success was needed to raise attention and strengthen the confidence that something significant could be done. Less articulated, but still important, was the idea that comprehensive, holistic development is a long-term goal which can only be reached step by step in phases. For the purpose of international advocacy, clear though limited goals were formulated. Efforts to reach these goals were supported by wide-ranging mobilization involving sectors of civic society which were not usually called upon to participate in attempts to enhance child welfare.

UNICEF began to focus on the reduction of infant mortality rates as a deliberate target for initiatives for which primary health care and basic services provided the foundation. In some countries, mostly in Africa, infant mortality rates were close to 200 per 1000 live births, and rates close to 150 were not uncommon in Africa and Asia; the average among all developing countries was 100. These high rates were a strong indication of social malaise, although they were in fact lower than the rates prevailing in many industrial countries during the nineteenth century and even at the beginning of the twentieth century.[11]

UNICEF saw a strategic value in establishing the reduction of infant deaths as a target behind which governments and their partners in the international community could rally. Such a target was both politically appealing and politically neutral and it would foster a constructive international competition to try to meet the ethical standards emerging around child issues in the late twentieth century. This approach was based on the idea that the promotion of a handful of primary health care techniques would favour other efforts which would in turn provide an entry point for the eventual realization of the entire primary health care package. While such a scheme had not been practicable in the past, the rapid spread of non-formal educa- tion and the accompanying social structures and of communications net- works, particularly radio and television, had now rendered it appropriate. UNICEF argued 'that the combination of political will and public dissemina- tion could achieve a critical mass, that the necessary information about pri- mary health care techniques could reach mothers and families with enough persuasiveness for them not only to want to use them, but even to demand them'.[12] This was eventually labelled the 'demand approach'.

These considerations resulted in the formulation of the 'GOBI initiative', which combined nutrition programmes, especially growth monitoring (G); oral rehydration therapy (O) to fight the worst killer of children, diarrhoea- induced dehydration; the restoration of breastfeeding (B); and immunization (I) against the major infectious childhood diseases. With the exception of the promotion of breastfeeding, the GOBI initiative was basically technology dri- ven, since the techniques relied on recent innovations and new forms of man- agement. To the original four programme areas were later added family planning and female literacy.

Growth monitoring focuses on the early diagnosis and treatment of malnu- trition. It is designed to complement the communication between mother and child by periodically dramatizing physical messages about the nutri- tional status and the growth process of the child.

Oral rehydration was conceived to combat the rapid and dangerous loss of fluids that often turns diarrhoea among children into a deathtrap. Some of the oral rehydration techniques are based on recent innovations; others have their roots in local practices. All are fairly easy to apply and with some instruction can be managed in the home. Oral rehydration was meant to be a bridging exercise within more long-term efforts to improve the hygienic environment of the child through access to safe water and the use of better health care methods and practices among caregivers. However, it has some- times been perceived as though UNICEF intended it as an alternative to long- term programmes, especially for financially strapped governments, because it appears to be an easy and financially attractive technology fix. However, even as an interim method, oral rehydration is dependent on the involve- ment and responsible engagement of people and governments at all levels, a well-functioning communication and outreach capacity and the cooperation of the private sector.

Breastfeeding offers nature's own combination of optimum nutrition and effective immunization during infancy that does not require any new tech- nology or accompanying investment. However, wherever female labour force participation rates are substantial or wherever business interests have contributed to a decline in the practice of breastfeeding through the promotion of breastmilk substitutes, large-scale social and institutional changes are needed to implement a breastfeeding programme. In this case, the achievement of a limited objective requires the support of broad-based endeavours engaging a combination of individual, community and institutional actors.

Eventually, most of the advocacy and operational energy of the GOBI initiative was directed toward immunization, which became the dominant element in the selective primary health care approach of the 1980s. The programme involved undertaking or increasing the substantial organizational efforts required to distribute, preserve and administer vaccinations. The recent success in eradicating smallpox inspired the World Health Assembly to set the achievement by the year 1990 of the goal of 80 per cent coverage against six communicable childhood diseases in an expanded programme for immunization. UNICEF's participation, which intensified at the beginning of the early 1980s, revolved around the attempt to convince countries and organizations to take this important, preventive component of primary health care seriously.

In 1984, following an international advocacy campaign led by UNICEF, many nations began exploring new ways to step up local immunization programmes as well as their activities in other areas of primary health care, especially those related to oral rehydration therapy and breastfeeding. Donor countries rapidly enlarged their financial contributions for these programmes and activities. The commitment of actors outside the health care sector, particularly politicians and people in the communications media, was critical and greatly encouraged those more directly concerned with the massive practical work.

However, the emphasis on clearly focused methods and a limited set of time-bound goals represented a significant change with respect to the basic services strategy, which had been characterized by broader goals promoted through a narrower approach. This change contributed to the impression that UNICEF was now pursuing a limited set of global targets rather than the highly flexible, context-specific targets for which it had become recognized and appreciated. This impression often overshadowed the fact that the programmes for children carried out through UNICEF field offices continued to be the mainstay of the organization's support for countries. These programmes included efforts aimed at improving water systems and sanitation, education, primary health care, nutrition and care for disabled children, as well as capacity building and institution building in these major areas. There were also considerable regional variations in UNICEF operations. These variations depended on previous achievements and region- and country-specific conditions. The new focus was not meant to supplant such programmes, but to provide help in the articulation of goals, strengthen accountability, promote awareness and foster the application of management techniques based on the setting of precise objectives.

Adding to the negative impression was the fact that, although primary health care and child development projects in many countries benefited from the wider public attention on children generally which was encouraged by immunizations and from the 'reaching out' which they generated, the attention of personnel, especially during immunization drives and particularly in poor and institutionally weak countries, became directed at a few key priorities in health care; consequently, at least temporarily, other priorities and other areas suffered, and there was some disruption. Thus, it appeared to some professionals that UNICEF regarded the promotion of the four techniques as somehow separate from the promotion of primary health care and 'the failure to emphasize the all-important goal of "health for all" rang alarm bells' at the World Health Organization.[13]

Other voices expressed concern that the initiative was monofocal and exclusively top-down. Many of these observations came from the same quarters which, at a meeting of UNICEF's board in 1978, had complained that the organization's efforts were too thinly spread out and that there was a lack of clear goals. Five years later there was widespread suspicion that UNICEF had abandoned the aim of promoting comprehensive primary health care and other broad programmes. The counter-argument that the comprehensive and integrated target of primary health care could only be reached through phases was frequently not heeded, as was the argument that it was necessary to instil confidence by demonstrating that important gains in preventive child health care could be achieved fairly rapidly on a large scale, at a reasonable cost and with the available knowledge and capacity. Curiously, the frustrations were voiced mainly by academics and others in the industrialized countries, which already had large, comprehensive health care infrastructures. The support and the willingness to participate in a continuously unfolding process of incremental steps toward improved health care came largely from professionals in the South.

For its part, UNICEF did not adequately report on the wider and more long-term approach to the many environments of the child in health care, water and sanitation, education, urban programmes, emergencies and, increasingly, child rights being pursued within the organization's country programmes.

This often quite heated debate continued throughout the 1980s, sometimes leading to distrust between the proponents of the two views. The debate arose mostly because of oversimplifications, for which the responsibility must be shared by both camps. The proponents of more selective, incremental and large-scale measures were not successful in making it clear that the ultimate goal was so important and broad that it required a phased, step-by-step approach to achieve development for the whole child. The advocates of holistic, integrated approaches, on the other hand, failed to realize the need for time-bound targets around which political and public commitment could be mobilized.

Combining strategies

Despite the controversy, the strengthening of primary health care through immunization campaigns gained rapid acceptance among countries and yielded early and quite dramatic results in terms of coverage and reductions in the incidence of disease. Several factors were behind this widespread improvement, including leadership, low-cost techniques, social mobilization, outside support and political and public participation.[14]

One weak element to which UNICEF gave growing attention during the 1980s was the role of leadership. Leadership has generally been one of the most neglected areas in economic and social analysis, which tends to put the emphasis on broad social factors and hesitates to give much or any weight to the role of individuals. In contrast, most of the immunization campaigns relied heavily and usually critically (and sometimes uncritically) on two or three individuals. Often the head of state was directly involved and a key minister played a major role. At the local level, similar leadership qualities frequently had an important influence.

One of the most thoughtful and thorough assessments of the 'world health movement for children' during the 1980s and at the beginning of the 1990s was undertaken in Latin America under the direction of Carl Taylor, an outstanding proponent of primary health care and a widely recognized leader in the field of child health.[15] While stressing that its observations are only valid for the Americas, the assessment underlined that 'perhaps the most important lesson that emerged from our findings was the absolute need for integration of all preventive programmes as part of primary health care'.[16] It also stated the following as the first observation in a summary of conclusions.

> The expanded programme on immunization/polio programme, as part of primary health care systems, with sustained support to achieve tightly sequenced priorities and measurable goals, has contributed positively to overall strengthening of health systems in the Americas. In field interviews, positive responses were three times more numerous than negative responses…. Both EPI and non-EPI health service staff had more positive than negative responses.[17]

'Of special interest,' the assessment went on at another point, 'is the finding that the most positive impact [of the immunization/polio programme] was on social mobilization … to reach the people, both through mass media and in their homes.'[18]

The authors recommend that the lessons of these experiences, along with intersectoral cooperation, both of which have so far been the weakest links in the primary health care system, be assigned priority in the effort to achieve the sustained improvement of health services in the Americas.

It is important that social mobilization be carefully planned. It must create opportunities for the participation of major segments of civic society. Within the UNICEF strategy, social mobilization was also expected to lay the foundation for fuller participation by people within their communities. In the efforts at social mobilization, there was an understanding that one of the most crucial places, perhaps the most crucial one, in which development needed to be grounded was the space of the mind. The belief that 'life can be improved and circumstances changed by one's own action is both an end and a means of development itself and an essential prelude to political participation, to the struggle for land reform and economic justice and to new attitudes towards family size and a further fall of population growth'.[19]

Tarzie Vittachi has elaborated eloquently on this point.

> When we talk about a child survival and development revolution, we are talking about bringing about a mass ripening for change, about opening people's mental boxes in which habitual acceptance of a low level of health and a high rate of death among their children is locked up as socially or fatefully decreed inevitabilities. We are talking about transforming deeply inlaid attitudes and practices and helping people to see over the hill. What needs to be done then is to present new knowledge to people as a way to empower themselves to change their perception of 'normality' or 'inevitability'.[20]

Until the 1980s cost analysis in social development programmes was sporadic. For social mobilization, especially that aimed at garnering political support, the cost aspect had to be moved to the fore. Jolly points out that if the costs to any of the participating parties had exceeded what they judged to be reasonable, their involvement would have required either coercion or subsidies.[21] This would have made rapid progress impossible.

Outside agencies, especially UNICEF, the World Health Organization and some international non-government organizations served a catalytic and an operational role. Without such involvement, which led to a global consensus, the sharing of experiences and a constructive competition among countries, the immunization drives would most likely not have been undertaken and the impressive results, despite the weaknesses in the reporting of outcomes and the fluctuating prospects for sustainability, would probably not have been achieved.

It was considered important that the proposal of goals and strategies for development for children should not only be guided by the relative seriousness of problems, but also that they should represent 'do-able' propositions. 'Do-able' in this context meant, among other things, low costs. The emphasis on this criterion was intended to boost and reorient 'political will' towards more child-centred choices. The issue of 'do-ability' had been under discussion for quite some time and was regarded as critical for any strategy of social betterment. The new idea was that political will was usually the prisoner of pragmatism, which in most cases meant that costs had to be lowered.

These were important motivations, but they were not the only ones. It could not be only a question of cost and manpower, otherwise the argument would have been the cynical one that, for the poor, initiatives must be fewer and cheaper. Instead, low-cost, do-able strategies were seen as considered responses to an ethical challenge. Peter Adamson, the author of UNICEF's annual report *The State of the World's Children*, formulated this challenge in the words, 'Morality must march with capacity,'[22] echoing the words of Immanuel Kant that, in order to avoid the trap of utopian dreams, 'should' must be preceded by 'can'. This was a strong plea for effective action for the vulnerable and the poor, for whom the sophisticated plans emanating from the development industry remained irrelevant. A low-cost strategy may not be ideal, but at least it is a beginning, while one waits for the perfect infra-structure to be installed or for the reallocation of major resources to the development needs of children.[23]

Another overriding concern was the ambition to improve the situation of a large number of children. For this, coverage became crucial. It was one of the most important and most hotly argued elements of the debate on develop-ment for children in the 1980s.

Myers distinguishes among three major strategies for achieving coverage: expansion, explosion and association.[24] Scaling up through 'expansion' typically begins with the testing of a model on a small scale; the model is then adjusted and extended to other locations until the desired coverage has been attained. Scaling up through 'explosion' bypasses the pilot stage. Programme implementation starts on a large scale, usually with the implementation of one model in all parts of a country. A process of adjustment at the local level may eventually be undertaken in order to render the programme more responsive to social needs and enhance coverage still further in certain places. Scaling up through 'association' involves piecing together the cover-age obtained through several projects or programmes, each responding to the needs of a distinct part of the total population served.

In the immunization drives, the explosion model predominated. This 'big bang' method of achieving coverage was usually the product of a political decision within a country, often motivated by a desire to gain broad support or to build good will. Maximum coverage was sought in the shortest possible period of time. This was bound to backfire. In fact, the explosion methods which were initially chosen by many countries were in most cases modified into processes of expansion.

Despite the short time span for many of the immunization drives, most countries managed to include a minimum amount of capacity building, especially in management, without which the significant outcomes would have been impossible. Through constant modification and frequent dialogues among community members and health care personnel, understanding and involvement on both sides grew remarkably quickly. Because of this, the goal of achieving near universal coverage among children and their parents through repeated immunization contacts helped in many countries to strengthen health care systems and the political, professional and financial support for these systems.[25]

There were weaknesses, deficiencies and outright mistakes caused by the urge for speed and the ambition for scale. There is no doubt that in several cases records were doctored to satisfy superiors. In some instances, other components of health care services and possibly other programmes suffered because of the drop in attention, especially in countries where infrastructure was weak and health care personnel were a scarce resource. Furthermore, the energy and enthusiasm generated in the worldwide race against time were difficult to maintain over long periods. The potential for reinforcing the organizational and management capacities of people and communities was also largely missed or neglected during the immunization drives which put the major emphasis on national and political mobilization.

Structural adjustment

Starting in the mid-1980s, UNICEF began to direct the attention of the world to the detrimental effects on children of the persistent global recession and the financial policies aimed at fostering economic adjustment in developing nations. Richard Jolly, who had been appointed as the UNICEF deputy executive director of programmes in 1981, had become increasingly concerned about the effects on children of the efforts to reach fiscal stability in poor countries. He agreed with the overall ambitions of these efforts, but disagreed strongly that the burden should be borne by the weakest segments of society, the children and the women.

Turning Alexander Dubček's phrase 'socialism with a human face', which had been suggested by one of his colleagues, into 'adjustment with a human face' and armed with cogent arguments, he more or less single-handedly initiated a tough discussion with the World Bank and the International Monetary Fund. UNICEF's board and the UNICEF executive director supported him. He was joined by very able economists, including Giovanni Andrea Cornia, Frances Stewart and Rolph van der Hoeven. Together, they undertook a survey of IMF-sponsored adjustment policies in ten countries. The results were employed to produce in 1984 a negotiating paper for the discussions with the IMF. The paper was not published until 1991. A quotation from the paper offers an indication of the arguments Jolly and his colleagues used.

> A recent study sponsored by UNICEF provides clear evidence of the extent and nature of such deterioration [in the welfare of women and children]. The study, comprising ten national case-studies from different types of developing countries, documents the severe and almost general decline in resources available to children, from both family resources and government allocations to the social sector. The decline in the quantity and quality of basic needs and social services offered appear to be very general. The impact on child survival and welfare appears to be widespread, especially in Africa and Latin America. Risk of death for children has increased in those cases where declines in household incomes and cuts in health services have been particularly acute. This has been observed recently in the plantation sectors of Sri Lanka and in Costa Rica.[26]

The initiative led to an intensive discussion, especially among economists. There is little doubt that this was the starting point for the broadening of the development debate that ultimately led to the launch by the UN Development Programme of its annual *Human Development Report*. It also led to a statement by then Chairman de Larosière of the IMF that is worth quoting.

> The extent to which adjustment is compatible with growth and with an improvement in living standards depends in large part on what form that adjustment takes. Adjustment that takes the form of increases in exports, savings, investment and economic efficiency will clearly be more supportive of growth than that which relies on cuts in investment and in imports. Similarly, adjustment that pays attention to the health, nutrition and educational requirements of the most vulnerable groups is going to protect the human condition better than adjustment which ignores them. This means that the authorities will have to be concerned, not only with IF they close the fiscal deficit but also HOW they do so.[27]

UNICEF's initiatives generated considerable interest both publicly and in government circles. They also led to an impressive series of research projects by universities, international agencies, non-government organizations and even governments. Some countries made policy changes to counter the negative impact of the harsh measures of fiscal discipline. However, from a practical perspective and from the point of view of women and children in the South, the assessment of the results must necessarily be modest. With the benefit of hindsight it is obvious that some rhetorical battles were won by UNICEF and that greater sensitivity toward the plight of vulnerable groups was created among the powerful collective financial institutions of the world. However, in reality the benefits for the poor, for the unemployed and for women and children were minimal. These people had never been considered in the massive lending offensive initiated by the big moneylenders flush with petrodollars in the 1970s. They had never heard the battlecry of the former chairmen of City Bank of New York that their countries would be the new and profitable clients of the financial world 'because states cannot go bankrupt'. In the end these people were the ones who were forced to carry the burden created by the monumental irresponsibility of the unholy alliance between the bankers of the rich countries and the elite of the poor countries. And they continue to do so to this day, but in poorer health, with less education and surrounded by the social violence which always follows in the footsteps of poverty and destitution. Against this backdrop, the inability of world leaders to solve the so-called debt crisis continues to be one of the major scams and shams of this century.

The rights of the child

Inspired by one of the most committed activists for children in modern times, Nils Thedin of Sweden, who seized on a Polish initiative to produce a special international convention to protect children, UNICEF belatedly, but then wholeheartedly, joined in the preparation of the Convention on the Rights of the Child, a document with a pedigree going back to Eglantyne Jebb and the adoption by the League of Nations of the Declaration on the Rights of the Child in the early 1920s.

There had been considerable resistance within UNICEF to the idea that it should devote its organizational energy and prestige to the drafting of a document which in the end might mean very little. Much of the work to overcome this resistance was carried out by Victor Soler Sola and the staff of the UNICEF Geneva office. In the process, the whole of UNICEF and its leadership were mobilized and the contents of the Convention significantly improved.

However, most of the credit both for the initiative and for the completion of the long, drawn-out negotiating and drafting process, which lasted ten years, must go to the numerous voluntary organizations and committed individuals who, with or without official national or international affiliation, persisted in their effective advocacy for a special convention on child rights.

Despite the many compromises and weaknesses which an internationally negotiated 'moral' document necessarily contains, the Convention has already become a very important tool for the protection of children, the promotion of their rights and the betterment of their conditions.

UNICEF has not yet clearly defined the role it wishes to play – or, as an intergovernmental organization, it will be allowed to play – among the many partners involved in the promotion, implementation and monitoring of the Convention. The very active part the organization has taken in the exceptionally rapid and nearly universal ratification of the Convention has been a very honourable contribution indeed. UNICEF is also increasingly using the articles of the Convention to guide its participation in joint planning with governments on programmes for children in countries where it has a presence. Likewise, the Convention has begun to serve as a mission state-ment for international children's organizations. UNICEF is also actively – mainly behind the scenes – supporting the international committee estab-lished to oversee the compliance of countries with the articles of the Conven-tion and to facilitate progress in the implementation of these articles. Among the methods UNICEF is employing to accomplish this is the support it is offering to the international committee for travel so that the committee can become familiar with the specific and varied conditions in countries. All these activities constitute first steps in a new role for UNICEF in the long and difficult effort to promote and implement the rights of the child.

Broadening the approach

Boldened by what it conceived to have been a decade of successful work, UNICEF decided to revive the ambitions of the International Year of the Child by supporting the Jomtien Conference on Universal Primary Educa-tion in 1989 and the First World Summit for Children in 1990; both of which contributed greatly to strengthening the international support for a broad-based approach to development for children.

The phased, large-scale strategy had been successful in deepening public awareness and strengthening the commitment to children within countries and at the international level. This also meant that a new opportunity had been created for addressing the more complex issues which had emerged because of the basic services concept. The regionally and globally negotiated goals for child-related development during the 1990s reflect this change. Through the World Declaration on the Survival, Protection and Development of Children and the related plan of action, the World Sum-mit for Children in 1990 pledged UNICEF to the adoption of a more integrated basic services strategy which recognized the interrelationships among the problems facing children and built on the experiences of the GOBI initiative in mobilizing all segments of society to achieve large-scale cover-age.

This was made possible, as UNICEF had predicted, by the positive results of the selective efforts to deal with major problem areas within the broader spectrum of the primary health care needs of children. Symbolized by the immunization drives, these efforts suggested that success in selected large-scale undertakings could become the groundwork for realizing all the other, equally important, components of the globally endorsed strategy. The ratio-nale was that, if substantial resources, energies, advocacy and supportive political choices could be applied in one significant area, the ability to address other child health needs would also be strengthened.

A critical factor in the strategy was the decision to establish time-bound and concrete targets to energize action, raise efficiency and nurture account-ability. This was reflected in the declaration and plan of action adopted by the World Summit for Children. Thus, in 1990 virtually all countries agreed to achieve seven major goals for child survival, development and protection by the year 2000. These goals include the reduction of the infant mortality rate and the under-five mortality rate each either by one-third, or, if it is less, to, respectively, 50 and 70 per 1000 live births, the reduction of the maternal mortality rate by one-half, the reduction of severe and moderate malnutrition among under-five-year-olds by one-half, the realization of universal access to safe drinking water and sanitary human waste disposal, the attainment of universal access to basic education and the completion of primary education by at least 80 per cent of primary school-age children, the reduction of the adult illiteracy rate to at least one-half the 1990 level, with an emphasis on greater female literacy, and better protection for children in especially diffi-cult circumstances.

Fairly soon after the World Summit for Children however, the broader vision was narrowed down from a comprehensive strategy to assist nations and communities to deal with the major problems facing children to a strat-egy based on the accomplishment of a much more limited set of 'mid-decade' goals. This was a pragmatic and reasonable choice which reflected the still robust conviction that it is necessary to phase efforts and to work towards focused and 'do-able' short-term goals in order to refortify the commitment and the capacity to reach complex, long-term goals. However, it was also crit-icized.

In the opinion of many inside and outside UNICEF the mid-decade goals, although justified from a viewpoint of management, reflected once more the same top-down approach which dominated the efforts to achieve universal child immunization. It created the impression that the guiding principle was to select problems which lent themselves to mainly technical interventions, thereby restricting the opportunity to deal with the broader issues. The approach to such issues – it was argued – should be founded on the under-standing of the embeddedness of the child and child-related problems in the overall social, political and economic environment.

The challenge now is to build on the positive achievements of large-scale, but still technically limited, approaches and seek to make broader and deeper inroads into the major problems of hunger and malnutrition, deficient health, poor hygiene and abuses of the rights of the child. In short, the challenge for the years ahead is to support countries and communities to make an all-out effort to plan and implement effective primary health care, relevant basic ser-vices including education for all and the translation of the Convention on the

Rights of the Child into reality. To realize these ambitions, communities, governments, voluntary organizations and international agencies must enter into new partnerships and jointly take on responsibilities for the betterment of the conditions of children and the environment of childhood. This requires mutual support among families, community members, non-government and activist organizations, concerned professionals and a caring state which relies increasingly on competent and committed representatives at all levels.

Knowledge and learning as priorities for the future

There is presently a broadening interest in UNICEF to transform itself from a programme and supply delivery agency into what is being called a 'knowledge organization'. The impact of UNICEF's cooperation is anticipated to be much greater if UNICEF provides ideas, relevant expertise and international experience of best practice to increase the knowledge base, improve capacity and build consensus for development for children. This is a healthy ambition. However, great care has to be taken so that this new orientation does not become a fashionable slogan promoted without the necessary analysis and insights into what it implies. Questions such as what kind of knowledge, knowledge about what, knowledge for whom and about relevant capacity and competence need to be raised and seriously pursued. Awareness must be created that the knowledge organization will not simply be seen as a repository of the ready-made bits of knowledge that can be applied as pre-made packages. In some circumstances – when problems are truly universal in nature and the best remedy is a technical intervention – global approaches may be justified. In most circumstances, however, tools and strategies and their application and adaptation have to be situation-specific. UNICEF can hope to become an effective knowledge organization only if it is willing to transform itself into a learning organization. The latter reflects the dynamism, interaction, and the constant adaptation needed to make well-informed choices at various stages of an ever ongoing and changing work.

There are other compelling reasons for making this distinction.[28] The practice of development cooperation is probably one of the most complex activities undertaken. It takes place amid rapidly changing and radically unpredictable social events, involving many actors with conflicting and competing interests, and ambitions, under intense and often hostile public scrutiny. There is no market for the product and hence the feedback is far from clear-cut. There is no price system that signals whether the product is in demand or not. The conditions in development assistance resemble those described in studies of complexity. Uncertainty about goals and objectives, the uncertainty of feedback mechanisms, the inequality, and often strong cultural differences between actors combine to increase the transaction cost in development cooperation. It is especially in situations of these kinds, which are turbulent and difficult to predict, that learning needs are highest. However, development agencies rarely have the structure, working processes and cultures most conducive to learning.

Furthermore, participants are mostly part of a national administrative environment or, in the case of the multilateral institutions, moulded on bureaucratic forms of organization. These are largely designed as stable hierarchies, primarily built to operate effectively under conditions of gradual change, reasonable certainty and a benevolent environment. They were seldom designed to deal with turbulence and chaos. Rapidly changing, complex and turbulent environments require different forms of organization. As Forss et al. have pointed out 'there would, therefore, seem to be a mismatch (at a very general level) between the task of development co-operation, and the government organisations as well as international agencies who are among the main actors'.[29]

For these reasons, and in order to take full advantage of emerging opportunities for locating children at the centre of policy and policy-making, UNICEF will need to develop a flexible, adaptable, creative and diversified approach to programming. This will demand changes intended to facilitate organizational learning. This, in turn, will require staff with high professional qualifications and experience, who can understand and manage change, who are committed to children's rights and sympathetic to issues and concerns for equity; a staff with excellent communications and negotiations skills who can undertake political, economic and social analysis.

By responding to these challenges in a constructive and imaginative way UNICEF can – in spite of limited financial and personnel resources – assist in shaping relevant and pragmatic, child-centred and rights-based social policies in the countries of the world. The gradual transformation of UNICEF and its country offices into a learning organization along the lines discussed here – with accompanying support from its Regional Offices and from its Headquarters – will have to be a top priority for the future.

Notes and references

1. Black (1986). Unfortunately Black's contribution to UNICEF's 50th anniversary was not available at the time of writing.
2. Black (1986), page 201.
3. For a recent discussion of the much needed transition from 'isolated' community participation to strategies of broad-based partnerships, see Korten and Alfonso (1983), Korten and Siy (1989), Uphoff (1992) and Taylor *et al* (1995).
4. Black (1986), page 205.
5. Black (1986), page 210.
6. Black (1986), pages 211ff.

7. Black (1986), page 350.
8. Prominent among the early pioneers was James Yen, who in the 1920s and 1930s developed the Ting Hsien experiment in China. This experiment was followed up by C.C. Chen and by John Grant. Grant continued with local colleagues to develop models for primary health care in India and Finland. Inspiration and experiences also came from the Gandhian movement and from the international work of the Christian Medical Commission. Carl Taylor of Johns Hopkins University has played a pivotal role in broadening the basis of competence and commitment to primary health care through a combination of field research and educational efforts attracting students from all over the world, many of whom have become national leaders in health care. Halfdan Mahler brought extensive field experience to his tasks as director general of WHO and worked energetically to change fundamental attitudes in medical establishments relative to the goals of primary health care.
9. Black (1986), page 350.
10. Black (1986), page 469.
11. See Corsini and Viazzo (1993), pages 9ff.
12. Black (1986), pages 470ff.
13. Black (1986), page 478.
14. Jolly (1993).
15. PAHO (1995).
16. PAHO (1995), page 10.
17. PAHO (1995), page 2.
18. PAHO (1995), page 10.
19. UNICEF (1995b), page 72.
20. UNICEF (1995b), page 72.
21. Jolly (1993), page 22.
22. See UNICEF (1987), pages 1ff.
23. Knutsson (1985).
24. Myers (1992), pages 379ff.
25. PAHO (1995).
26. Helleiner, Cornia and Jolly (1991), page 1825.
27. Cornia, Jolly and Stewart (1987), page 2.
28. For this discussion I am indebted to Forss, Cracknell and Stromquist (1997).
29. Forss, Cracknell and Stromquist (1997), page 3.

Part II

Learning from the debate: the need for change

The discussion on the environments of the child, the glimpses of various perceptions about them and some lessons from the debate on children and the efforts at international cooperation on their behalf now lead us to ask some difficult questions about what we need to do to improve our knowledge and our understanding of development and children. The following are some of these questions.

- How can we improve our theories and methods of inquiry, especially in social studies, so that knowledge about children and childhood and the environments in which they live and interact becomes trustworthy and relevant, and so that our understanding of problems and their underlying causes becomes adequate?
- How can a deeper understanding of the ideology of development help push the focus of development towards human betterment and assist us in efforts to include children and childhood in the economic and political calculus?
- What are some of the political and practical steps which need to be taken in order to transform the Convention on the Rights of the Child into reality for children?

Essay 6: Tools for a better understanding

The previous essays in this collection have examined some of the traits of the debate on children and of the efforts to better their situation. Here and there in this review we have indicated paths along which our thinking and our practice need to proceed. However, if we wish, as we should do, to move away from inherited perceptions and assumptions, sometimes uncritically accepted, towards firmer insights, we must ask ourselves about the additional changes which we need to promote in the debate on betterment for children.

The ambition should not be to propose a new and presumably grand theory of development for children. Such a theory is neither desirable, nor possible; there can be no one theory about the manifold problems, purposes and processes which have been considered under the various umbrellas of development. Rather, some key principles which can guide future approaches towards strategies truly incorporating children, in theory and in practice, must be identified. The recommendations put forward here represent proposals of a theoretical, ethical and strategic nature which ought to be considered. We need, for example, to address several fundamental questions about the ways in which our knowledge about children and about development is produced and how it can be improved. Clearly, any such attempt requires a rethinking of the broad and basic assumptions of social theory that influence or determine our ability to understand the conditions and the problems of children and childhood.

A striking impression emanating from our review of the nature of the debate about children and betterment for children revolves around the urgency of the need to improve our knowledge from the perspective of children and about children as social actors during the various significant phases of childhood, in relation to other children and to adults, in their immediate environment and in wider contexts and different institutional settings. To accomplish this will require studies and research about children

95

and with children on their experiences, their understanding and their migration into ever broadening social and cultural arenas. Students of social studies will have to reeducate themselves in new approaches. Like all pioneering efforts, this research will not be easy; but where it has been tried, as in Parana, a low-income settlement outside Brasilia, or in urban areas in Kenya, it has proven a valuable complement to conventional fieldwork and survey approaches and has provided crucial insights for the analysis and understanding of broader problems.[1]

Work with children offers important and as yet largely untapped opportunities for a better understanding of specific child-related problems, as well as of the ongoing construction and reproduction of society. Respect for the perspective of children in the various phases of childhood is not only necessary in social and cultural studies for practical reasons and in the light of the right of children to participate and be heard. It may also prove to be as enriching and rewarding in general theoretical and practical terms as the choice of the perspective of women has been during the last few decades.

To be able to broaden social knowledge in these directions, we must be aware of how such knowledge is produced and how this affects our perceptions and our understanding of children and childhood. As a starting point, we have to recognize that, although any definition of reality may turn out to be a combination of projected perceptions (a sociological version of quantum theory), for practical purposes people live and act, not in an economy, polity or religion or in any other analytically constructed compartment, but in a total 'reality room' which has all of these aspects. Our 'realities' are separated into sectoral entities only because of the observer's urge for classifications and intellectual orderliness. In real life they are aspects of a total web of images and activities which we constantly traverse, combine and interpret. Our total 'reality room' has physical walls and walls of technology, knowledge and organization, as well as paintings of meaning and value. This must be remembered when we try to understand the nature of the descriptive models, the explanatory normative models which we construct of reality for the purpose of knowing, understanding and making use of it. Problems of human deprivation and proposals to overcome them must begin with an understanding of their location within all the dimensions of human reality. An example can help guide our thinking.

A mother in a village in the province of Punjab in Pakistan is giving birth. She is assisted by her mother, her sister and a traditional birth attendant. The birth attendant has received a little training at the district health centre, but relies mostly on what has been handed down to her by previous generations of women. The required ceremonies have been performed, labour begins. When the child appears, special attention is given to the colour of the skin. If there has been any obstruction in the supply of oxygen and the child is discoloured, little is done, for the child has been the victim of the 'evil eye'. If the child does not recuperate on its own, it is left to succumb without any remedial action. In the case of the mother in Punjab, the birth is not endangered by such perils, so the umbilical cord is cut and ashes from the fireplace are applied. The birth attendant is aware of the risks of tetanus infection and is careful to apply ashes taken from the centre of the hearth. There – she has been told – the ashes are clean and can be used as the age-old welcoming sign taken from the symbolic centre of the household.

The risks for a child and its mother on the occasion of birth must be understood and managed in relation to the physical context in which it takes place and the technology used by birth attendants and others who help. However, equally important are the social recognition and support provided to the mother and those who are assisting her, the knowledge applied, and the values and the perceptions of the meaning of life which are shared and respected within the mother's social and cultural environment.

We must adopt the attitude of Karl Popper when he advised his readers that, 'We are not students of any subject matter, we are students of problems.'[2] Consequently, safe motherhood and the threats to both mother and child in the absence of safe practices are not biological, medical, technological, organizational or educational issues. They are issues with all these aspects. Only by thoroughly realizing the meaning and the implications of this can we perceive the fallacies and distortions caused by the sectoralization of knowledge.

Differences in the accessibility of knowledge

These insights, illustrated by the use of the metaphor of the 'reality room', can educate us on how we might achieve knowledge about the various layers of a problem and their respective relevance for action. If we look at the important issue of safe motherhood, which is crucial for the survival and well-being of women and children, it is fairly easy to describe and evaluate the hygienic hazards to a safe delivery and the well-being of mother and child. It is much more difficult to excavate and examine the deeply ingrained patterns of knowledge and the elusive, but forceful, features of norms and values that need to be analysed and, if necessary, altered to achieve a lasting betterment of health or any other condition of children.

These differences in the accessibility and in the interpretation of relevant factors increase the risk that we will fill in the gaps with our own knowledge or with unreflected assumptions and thereby distort both understanding and communication.

The question of time

Our metaphor of the 'reality room' can help us recognize that different social and cultural spaces also represent various dimensions of social and cultural 'time'. In the management of the physical environment and of technology, people may respond fairly rapidly to changed requirements. Social structures, on the other hand, are related to time and to change in different ways. The age-old caste system, closely tied to centuries-old patterns of stratification and patron–client relationships in rural India, is still thriving. Presently, it is actually being reinforced, as it is merged with the more modern hierarchy of economic and social classes in industrialized India. Even in its modernized version it provides a very powerful social and mental framework for perceptions, aspirations and interactions.

To account for such differences, concepts like 'cultural lag' have been fashioned to explain what appears to be inconsistencies or inertia, as if time in some parts of the 'reality room' were moving in a different and slower motion than the day-to-day world. We must observe and consider in theory, as well as in practice, that the passage of time and the flow of change are not uniform processes. It is as if there were several separate dimensions of time in social and cultural space. There seems to be a physical time operating in the physical and technological dimensions of the 'reality room'. Here we seem to relate and respond fairly rapidly to challenges arising from a changing environment or the introduction of, for example, new technologies. However, in order to manage significantly changed situations successfully, we need to create or adjust our structural and institutional tools. This requires much more time. Therefore the organizational and structural time dimensions are different – more extended and more lethargic – from changes in the physical and technological environments. Structures and institutions have their own history and their own inertia.

For similar reasons, we must also consider significant and culturally codified knowledge as a separate space in which time has very special characteristics. We could call this 'normative' time. This time seems to move at a much lower speed than time in the other dimensions of the reality room. This is especially visible when values and norms are anchored in religion and thus, in principle, regarded as being above or beyond the changes which we feel we can control and manage through our own actions.

Reflections on issues like these are rarely found in problem analysis or for that matter in practical descriptions. This must change. In the management of birth in Punjab, we note that the handling of some technical aspects have improved. However, where knowledge is strong and firmly institutionalized, as in the case of the evil eye and its manifestations in the newborn, the nature and consequences of the time dimension is quite different. Old knowledge is still regarded as valid. Unless we understand this and use the understanding, we will not be able to better the situation.

Understanding change

To manage changing conditions, whether originating inside or outside one's society, one must control a critical level of resources, whether technical, economic, or organizational, or in terms of knowledge and ambitions.

Here, the model of the 'reality room' can help our understanding. It contains all the resources required – not just the technical and economic ones which dominate typical perceptions of 'development' – and the combination of assets, tangible or otherwise, which are needed to make good use of new opportunities. Depending on the situation, the nature of these assets will vary, but they will necessarily be multidimensional, like the total 'reality room'. If some of these assets are lacking, be they physical, technological, economic or political, or consisting of the mental resources of knowledge, beliefs, aspirations or values, the successful management of change will be severely hampered. Two very brief stories show the importance of management control in all these dimensions.

In Dhaka, Bangladesh, Razia, a 14-year-old girl and the daughter of a low-income civil servant, attends secondary school. Her next door neighbour and friend is of the same age. This friend is the daughter of a much wealthier grain trader. Despite the wealth of her family, the friend stopped going to school after the fourth grade and spends most of her time helping her mother with chores. Though the money, the social status and the other assets for sending children to school are available in the friend's family, the crucial asset of a supportive perception which appreciates gender equity and the need to allow women to seize new opportunities is lacking.

In a village outside Comilla in Bangladesh, the manufacture of concrete slabs to cover pit latrines is providing a new source of income. Nonetheless, the village's own latrines are the same old contraptions: bamboo platforms – covered for privacy – that stretch out over the village stream and increase the already high level of toxins and bacteria. Infections and diarrhoea are common. The desire, knowledge and technology necessary to improve sanitation exist. Economically, however, the solution is out of reach.

Even these highly compressed accounts point to the need for a new conceptual framework for our reflections on the social and cultural contexts in which the problems of children and childhood are embedded.

Fredrik Barth has combined common sense, extensive fieldwork and philosophical insights to arrive at similar views. His underlying ambition is the same: to find theoretical tools and methodical approaches which can help us to capture the 'totality' of human reality and at the same time to distinguish meaningfully among the various factors on which we need to focus in our reflections, as well as in our actions. We need to manage this double-edged ambition in such a way that the challenges which it poses are neither mystified nor oversimplified. He writes:

> I assume that there is a real world out there, but that our representations of that world are constructions. People create and apply these cultural constructions in a struggle to grasp the world, relate to it and manipulate it through concepts, knowledge and acts. In the process, reality impinges, and the events that occur consequently are not predicated by the cultural system of representations employed by the people, though they may largely be interpretable within it. A people's way of life is thus not a closed system, contained within their own cultural constructions. That part of the real world on which we as anthropologists need to focus is composed of this widest compass: a natural world, a human population with all its collective and statistical social features, and a set of cultural ideas in terms of which these people try to understand and cope with themselves and their habitat.[3]

Popper and Eccles have made similar attempts to identify what may constitute the fundamental resources on which we can draw for our construction of reality.[4] They suggest a classification based on 'three worlds': the world of the physically given ('world 1'), the world of mental operations ('world 2') and the world of mental artifacts or the images exchanged, traded and often inherited in a 'cultural' tradition ('world 3'). These 'worlds' roughly overlap with the major dimensions in the description of man's 'reality room'.

Explicitly and implicitly, Barth, Popper and Eccles warn against the uncritical application of content-oriented concepts and classifications. These tend to 'freeze' what in reality is a constantly changing flow of images and a continuum of perceptions. Because of this, we tend to look at our concepts as boxes that contain a specific part of reality. This is the way in which we commonly think and talk about societies, communities and cultures, states, nations, ethnic groups and markets, as if they were in separate boxes instead of as changing constellations of numerous interrelated and interrelating factors. One is reminded of Myrdal's critique of economic and social theory.

> our conceptual boxes are empty primarily because they are not built in such a way that they can hold reality. We need new theories, which, however abstract, are more realistic in the sense that they are in a higher degree adequate to the facts.[5]

Up to now few steps have been taken to remedy these deficiencies. We still tend to favour concepts that place the emphasis on content and somehow suggest that the boundaries inherent in the classifications which we make correspond to similar arrangements in empirical reality. This in fact is a metaphysical assumption and can create great difficulties when we try to understand the reasoning and behaviour of ordinary people who are not constrained in their thoughts or actions by such theoretical biases.

In sum, we need a deeper understanding of man's social and cultural 'reality' that is theoretically and analytically more helpful than what has been offered by various schools of social thought thus far. We also need to search for ways of bridging the widening gap between human experience and scientific abstraction. The possibilities are there, if we dare to address fundamental, epistemological and conceptual problems in the study of society and in our reflections about the nature of human reality. It is in this spirit that a strategy needs to be designed which reflects the integrated nature of human experience and which allows us to focus on more specific problems by using a 'dimensional' or 'perspective' approach for the understanding of the nature of man's total 'reality room'.

Only if we dare to abandon oversimplified patterns of sectoralization and disaggregation can we minimize the damage created by distorted knowledge and move towards new and more fruitful insights which can also help us identify ways to approach childhood, the conditions of children and the nature of the problems facing children with a greater chance of a reliable understanding and a relevant and meaningful practice.

The complementarity of theory and practice

The situation of children and the problems they are facing are multi-dimensional and complex. This demands 'complementarity' and mutual supportiveness in our approaches to theory and practice rather than either-or solutions. Bridges between theory and practice therefore need to be constructed so that we can reach a more reliable knowledge base for deepened understanding and for relevant, meaningful and sustainable action.

Important chasms have characterized the public debate on children for a considerable time. One of the major chasms has been caused by a fundamental difference in perceptions, understanding and priorities which depends on the perspectives from which a child-related issue is contemplated. In thinking about a problem one is expected to ponder a great number of factors affecting the situation of the child. In action, selectivity is required, since only a limited number of issues can reasonably be managed in a practical endeavour. For these reasons, programme proposals are bound to be narrower than theoretical considerations and they often tend to be judged deficient when more holistic standards are applied. Thus, academics often criticize projects for 'monofocality' and lack of awareness. They view a practical perspective as mechanical, simplistic and exhibiting little concern for long-term outcomes and sustainability.

On the other hand, when persons of action evaluate wide-ranging theoretical proposals, the lack of pragmatic relevance and feasibility is lamented just as much. They criticize theoreticians for overtheorizing and accumulating knowledge only for the sake of knowledge. For similar reasons, reflective and questioning practitioners are dismissed as being 'philosophical' by colleagues who believe that the key to progress lies in a go-out-and-get-'em attitude and that a wrong decision is better than no decision at all. This chasm between the 'knowledge' community and the 'action' community has become a major source of disagreement and frustration.

A good example of this sort of controversy is offered by the prolonged and often heated discussion between UNICEF and the World Health Organization (WHO) over primary health care. WHO, a specialized agency, serves as the global coordinator and guardian of standards in health matters. It is staffed mainly by health professionals. Health managers have usually had their practical experience in comprehensive programmes of health research or in the administration of health systems. The dominant outlook within WHO emphasizes holistic approaches and assigns priority to the establishment of viable and functioning health care infrastructures. In contrast UNICEF was set up to assure a rapid response in emergencies. It was originally staffed mainly by practitioners. In recent decades the staff has become more specialized through the recruitment process and through internal training. Nevertheless, the tradition of rapid and effective response is still a strong ingredient in UNICEF's organizational culture. This is one of the reasons the UNICEF emphasis in both policy and practice over the years has been on pragmatic, large-scale programmes of action.

In the area of health, UNICEF has worked with WHO to evolve an approach to primary care. However, because of its orientation towards action and results, UNICEF has argued that broader goals can only be reached in phases involving incremental steps to achieve constructive outcomes and create the impetus for more commitment even before a satisfactory infrastructure has been created. Indeed, one of its major arguments has been that phased and selective approaches generating visible and appreciated results are needed in order to bypass structural weaknesses and convince concerned parties of the need ultimately to strengthen health care systems.

The position of WHO, on the other hand, has mainly been that, before major primary health care activities can be launched, governments need to be assisted in building, staffing and managing comprehensive systems of health facilities through which primary health care can be implemented and sustained. There can be no argument about this. A comprehensive health system supported by competent and adequate staff is certainly needed if primary health care is to succeed. Meanwhile, however, it is very unlikely that the required resources will be forthcoming if service efficiency has not already convinced politicians that the investment in staff and infrastructure is worthwhile.

The controversy between the two positions has been dominated by an either-or discourse, which in turn has been interpreted in terms of 'right' and 'wrong' and 'dos and don'ts'. In the future, more serious efforts must be made to clarify the fact that the two approaches are grounded in two equally justified and complementary theoretical and practical frameworks which, rather than segregated, need to be combined in feasible and pragmatic ways.

Some major perceptions representing critical differences between 'thinking' about problems and 'acting' to solve them can be illustrated by comparing the apparent preferences among observers and policymakers located at the theoretical end of the spectrum, where the complexities of issues are analysed, with the ambitions of people trying to achieve change as quickly as possible. The two clusters of perspectives and attitudes represent the two sides of a major faultline in perceptions, valuations, knowledge and approaches.[6] Despite the serious consequences emanating from it, this faultline is rarely discussed and few attempts are made to mend it; this further inflames the debate. The following diagram illustrates these problems.

At the 'theoretical' end of the spectrum there is a general tendency to pay special attention and assign a high value to:	At the 'action' end of the spectrum there is a corresponding tendency to concentrate on:
The theoretical-holistic nature of problems	Opportunities for action
The embeddedness of children and childhood in society and culture	Children mainly as individuals and targets for social action
Interdependencies among various aspects of child situations and between problems and needs	Crucial problems and priority needs
Recognition of cultural specificities	The universal characteristics of children and their needs
Broad goals	Focused goals
A combination of strategies on all levels of action	Technological strategies and supportive communication
The involvement of people in providing knowledge, formulating goals and implementing activities	The mobilization of people for specific goals
Building capacity	Utilizing capacity

A choice between these two major avenues would have important consequences on one's actions. However, the challenge is to avoid being trapped in simplistic 'either-or' approaches and instead recognize that the two streams of theory and practice can flow together and move forward through interaction and mutual support. Theoretical and practical approaches must both be based on respect for the complexity of problems. Initiatives should be guided by clear and well-grounded reasoning and not just by routine assumptions. The theoretical and practical perspectives should be seen as poles – not as opposites – and as mutually supportive approaches to the achievement of the goals.

Closely linked to these issues is the need to combine the description and assessment of situations, and problems affecting children, with a pragmatic analysis of various causative factors. For this UNICEF – guided by the work done by Urban Jonsson in Tanzania – has developed the so-called triple-A approach. It consists of assessment of observable symptoms and problems, analysis of different layers of immediate, underlying and basic causes behind the problems, and proposals for strategies of action emerging from the assessment and analysis. The outcome of the resulting programmes will be monitored with the intention of creating an iterative cycle of renewed and improved assessment, analysis and action. In so doing the ambition is to be able to go beyond the level of symptoms to the various causative factors generating them and to propose pragmatic and feasible strategies which can be used to deal with the immediate problems and with the critical determinants behind them. The methodology is an effective tool for understanding and addressing the linkages between existing structures and underlying generative processes and for bridging between different levels of analysis. Sensibly applied, it has become an important instrument for adpative, flexible and realistic programming, contributing to efforts to strengthen UNICEF as a learning organization.

Building bridges among disciplines

If one acknowledges that children are embedded in their social and cultural environments, it becomes obvious that our understanding and our action must be intersectoral and interdisciplinary. If the struggle against poverty, inequity and injustice is not vigorously pursued, betterment for children will not be forthcoming; if technologies are inhuman and ineffective, if unemployment is rampant, or if social, political and economic structures at the local and national levels are inadequate or oppressive, children will suffer. To face such broad challenges, approaches and their disciplinary underpinnings must be complementary and interactive, not exclusive or inward-looking.

Previous rather primitive attempts at an interdisciplinary approach responded to the ambition to do what one was trained to do, the only difference being that one tried to do it all at the same time. The result might be called 'parallel sectoral confusion'. Well-established research disciplines and well-known, uncontroversial methods were favoured over new research into social, cultural and environmental realities which requires much more time and theoretical openness and which lacks status among a technology-oriented and highly sectoralized intellectual establishment.

The interdisciplinary approach which began to emerge in the 1960s had certain advantages. It recognized the necessity of building on a broader understanding of the context of sectoral issues. As a result, attempts were made to undertake sequential analysis by proceeding from broader frameworks to the more specialized examination of inherent problems. However, a basic weakness of this approach was the isolation, both personal and analytical, among the people involved. Thus, the linkages between broader issues and more specialized issues and among the various phases of a cumulative effort at building knowledge did not emerge.

A much more mature view of interdisciplinary cooperation emerged in the 1970s. Proposed by anthropologists and scholars of the theory of science, this view focuses on an ongoing process of collective reinterpretation by teams of professionals who are sincerely committed to interdisciplinary cooperation and who apply their diverse and complementary skills to a common 'territory' of research.[7] The various specialists, while studying specific aspects of problems, are able to communicate by referring to the same 'reality' their counterparts in other fields refer to. This approach combines holistic and specialist contributions and generates a shared perspective both on the broader context and on the nature of the different 'sectoral components'.

An illustration of this method is provided by work in growth monitoring over the last 20 years. The growth-monitoring strategy still faces many serious difficulties because of widespread failure to translate all parts of the proposal into effective practice. Theoretically, however, it is quite unusual, since it is built on a combination of insights from anthropology, biology, linguistics, pædiatric nutrition, public health and systems theory that was developed by David Morley, Jon Rhode and others in the 1970s.

The strategy is designed to address the crisis which generally occurs among infants during the nutritional transition from breastfeeding to the intake of other food. Poor nutrition during this period in the lives of infants can have especially grave consequences on infants in countries where hygiene, health knowledge and nutritional practices are deficient and where child spacing is a problem. The crucial assumption behind the promotion of growth monitoring is that during this period of six months to two years there is a serious discrepancy between the change in nutritional requirements and the ability of the child to communicate with its environment, especially with its mother. As long as the supply of breastmilk is sufficient the baby's signals produce satisfactory responses. However, when the supply declines or is affected by other factors, the ability of the infant to communicate becomes inadequate and cannot produce a relevant feedback. Infections, diarrhoea, weight loss and dehydration are some of the results of this breakdown, which leads to nutritional and health impairment and, if unchecked, ultimately death. During this period there is an urgent need to strengthen the feedback loop and the mother's responses. Through the use of simple charts on which the infant's growth is plotted, growth monitoring has been designed to provide the mother with warning signals or communicate a signal that nutritional progress is satisfactory. A potentially risky nutritional situation caused by imbalances between nutritional requirements and the child's lack of adequate communication skills is addressed by complementing the latter, resulting in a 'linguistic' approach to a problem of health.

Notes and references

1. Hart (1992), page 17. Mutuku and Mutiso (1994), pages 335ff.
2. Cited in Hechter (1987), page viii. Myrdal's warning words to his colleagues in the social sciences and economics some forty years ago echo the same worries. They deserve to be repeated.

   > In reality there is, of course, no distinction between facts corresponding to our traditional scholastic divisions of social science into separate disciplines. A realistic analysis of problems can never stop at such lines of division. The distinction between factors that are 'economic' and those that are 'non-economic' is indeed a useless and nonsensical device from the point of view of logic and should be replaced by a distinction between 'relevant' and 'irrelevant' factors or 'more relevant' and 'less relevant'. And this latter dividing line should not be expected to be the same for different problems. Myrdal (1957), page 10.

3. Barth (1987), page 87.
4. Popper and Eccles (1977).
5. Myrdal (1957), page 168.
6. These differences bear a resemblance to the ones described in Essay 4 under 'positional perspectives'. However, they should not be confused with the latter. The rationales of the contrasting views vary and they are not tied to the 'geographical' or 'organizational' location of the observer.
7. Törnebohm (1974).

Essay 7: The need to rethink development

If we wish to learn from the debate on children, childhood and betterment for children, and resolve some of the problems it poses, we must consider the larger contexts relevant to the debate. There is no shortcut. We must scrutinize the intellectual and ideological environment which, whether we like it or not, conditions the debate. More particularly, if we wish to advocate – as we must do – for the inclusion of children within overall strategies and policies for development and accord them the attention they deserve in major development processes, we must discuss at least briefly the existing discourse on 'development'.

The concept of development is one of the oldest and most powerful of all Western ideas.[1] Its foundations go at least as far back as the perceptions of time in the Old Testament and include elements from Augustine, Renaissance writers and French philosophers like Condorcet and Turgot, who combined the idea of linear time with theories couched in terms of an ongoing improvement of technical and social conditions.

The concept of development began to take on its modern day tones when the sociological imitators of Wallace and Darwin proclaimed that Victorian Britain was the measure of the evolution of man and his society. Had Britain not conquered much of the rest of the globe? Ironically, Marx was perhaps the greatest development enthusiast of all with his fascination for social mechanics, although he emphasized the dimensions of human rights and ethics that unfortunately were abandoned by his followers and taken up later and most fervently by his detractors.

Since the Second World War, a substantial literature has sprung up on development theory. In the many overviews on the subject, four major schools are commonly identified. These revolve around what may be called the 'modernization', the 'dependency', the 'world system' and the 'alternative development' paradigms.[2] For all practical purposes modernization is equivalent to Westernization, since countries in the West have served as models of modernization for the rest of the world. From this perspective, development is mainly an imitative process. This view dominated the theoretical debate during the 1950s and 1960s and still conditions many of the perceptions upon which international aid programmes are based.

The dependency school has been very critical of the modernization theory, but not so very different in its conception of development. The most important obstacles to development are seen to be lack of capital and of entrepreneurial skills, which are external to the underdeveloped economy. The international division of labour is analysed in terms of relations among regions of the world, of which two – the centre and the periphery – assume particular importance. Because the periphery is deprived of its surplus, development in the centre somehow implies underdevelopment in the periphery. Thus, development and underdevelopment may be described as two aspects of a single global process. All regions participating in the process are defined as capitalist, but a distinction between central and peripheral capitalism can be made. Since the periphery is doomed to underdevelopment because of its dependence on the centre, it is considered necessary for a peripheral country to disassociate itself from the world market and strive for self-reliance.

Some of the tenets of the world-system theory are similar to those of dependency theory. According to this view, the world system is the result of the expansion over the last 500 years of European and later Western capitalism. Today, the political and cultural constellations associated with the free market economy are behind the accelerating globalization of the market. The world systems school has inspired a vast number of studies on the nature and impact of the various types of globalization.[3]

The most well-known alternative development proposal came from the Hammarskjold Foundation and its international network of supporters in the 1970s. In its critique of the modernization and Westernization school, the proposal built on elements from the dependency and world systems schools. It has inspired more recent efforts to achieve balanced economic development that have given prominence to basic needs and 'people-focused development'.

A more radical offspring of the alternative development perspective is the formulation of a 'green' alternative based on the values of cultural identity, self-reliance, social justice and ecological balance.[4] This alternative represents an attempt to capture and articulate emerging aspirations, ideas and practice among constituencies which have either been marginalized by technology-driven development or have consciously chosen to oppose it. It is also different in the sense that it is inductive rather than deductive and deterministic.[5]

These distinctions among development schools have been made many times in various ways by several authors, but they are rarely referred to in the debate on betterment for children. In the same vein, children are, with some few exceptions, conspicuous by their absence in the macroeconomic and political theories upon which the strategies and policies affecting children are based.[6] Although sometimes arguments are made about the critical role which genuine betterment, especially betterment in the health and education of children, plays in achieving goals within the economic sphere, most of the discussion on betterment for children has taken place outside the various theoretical contexts described here.[7]

The concept, ideology and rhetoric of development became part of the public rhetoric and later of everyday language in the 1950s. What really set it in motion was a skilful ploy: the invention of its opposite number, underdevelopment, which divided the world into the fortunate countries which were 'developed' and the footnote countries which were 'underdeveloped'. With a euphemistic twist, the latter were eventually called 'developing' countries, but the meaning is the same: they are behind and their task is to 'catch up' with those countries which have graduated. Meanwhile, the 'developed' countries kindly volunteer to provide models, tools, guidance and some marginal resources, so that the unlucky latecomers can begin to climb the ladder, basically on conditions set by the global centres of power.

Thus, 'underdevelopment' was promulgated on 20 January 1949 in Harry S. Truman's inaugural address. 'On that day,' writes Gustave Esteva, a former director of planning in the Mexican Government, 'two billion people became underdeveloped. In a real sense, from that time on, they ceased being what they were, in all their diversity, and were transmogrified into an inverted mirror of others' reality: a mirror that belittles them and sends them off to the end of the queue, a mirror that defines their identity, which is really that of a heterogeneous and diverse majority, simply in the terms of a homogenizing and narrow minority.'[8] Esteva continues with a clarity and energy which would be lost in any attempted summary.

> Since then, development has connoted at least one thing: to escape from the undignified condition called underdevelopment. When Nyerere proposed that development be the political mobilization of a people for attaining their own objectives, conscious as he was that it was madness to pursue the goals that others had set; when Rodolfo Stavenhagen proposes today ethno-development or development with self-confidence, conscious that we need to 'look within' and 'search for [our] own culture' instead of using borrowed and foreign views; when Jimoh Omo-Fadaka suggests a development from the bottom up, conscious that all strategies based on a top-down design have failed to reach their explicitly stated objectives; when Orlando Fals Borda and Anisur Rahman insist on participatory development, conscious of the exclusions made in the name of development; when Jun Nishikawa proposes an 'other' development for Japan – conscious that the current era is ending; when they and so many others qualify development and use the word with caveats and restrictions as if they were walking in a minefield, they do

not seem to see the counterproductivity of their efforts. The minefield has already exploded.... For two-thirds of the people of the world, underdevelopment is a threat that has already been carried out, a life experience of subordination and of being led astray, of discrimination and subjugation. Given that precondition, the simple fact of associating with development one's own intention tends to annul the intention, to contradict it, to enslave it. It impedes thinking of one's own objectives, as Nyerere wanted; it undermines confidence in oneself and one's own culture, as Stavenhagen demands; it clamours for management from the top down, against which Jimoh rebelled; it converts participation into a manipulative trick to involve people in struggles for getting what the powerful want to impose on them, which was precisely what Fals Borda and Rahman wanted to avoid.[9]

Like all large concepts, especially those which become fashionable, the concept of development is not only complex and difficult, it can also be dangerous. Its very broadness may hide rather than reveal what might be intended. The sanitizing nature of the term can effectively mask neocolonialism, economic dominance, dependency and other expressions of the imbalances in global economic and political power. In addition, the term has a tempting attractiveness. It sounds pleasing, linked as it often is to other similar and equally nebulous terms like 'internationalism', 'universalism' and 'globalization'.

This should not astonish us. It is in the nature of political slogans to allow many interpretations and thereby to combine conflicting views around some common, strongly felt values. Over time, development has acquired a number of meanings with which different constituencies can identify. It is generally considered synonymous with 'improvement' and 'progress'. It represents increased production, high material standards of living, improved control over resources, economic growth, food security, greater access and equality in the management of economic and political systems, literacy, the enhancement of knowledge, greater equity in the distribution of resources and many other things which are considered good by people at large or by specific interest groups.

This openness in the concept, which may also be viewed as a fundamental theoretical weakness, has provided the common rhetorical framework and idiom used by many newly independent nations to articulate their aspirations for a better future. For those who define themselves as 'developed', it legitimizes the identification, evaluation and prescription of major economic and political goals for economically less well-off countries.[10] Like other concepts of a similar nature, 'development' has been aggregated to a level where it seems to have taken on a life of its own. Phrases like 'development requires...', 'we need to develop...', and 'in order to develop...' are used as if they were references to something which surely exists beyond all question for all people throughout the world.

Many times it is useful to be able to employ a broad concept in order to orient ourselves and readily place an area or a topic within a context. This is legitimate. However, it is also quite different from allowing such concepts to dominate our analysis and guide our action. Indeed, it is puzzling that a concept which has sprung from the discarded theoretical framework of the philosophical optimism and social evolutionism of 150 years ago can continue to dominate our discussions, analyses and actions. It is even more puzzling that this can go on in spite of widespread awareness of the weaknesses of the concept and the strong ethnocentric, political and economic bondage of the term to a particular situation in a specific historical phase of industrial society.

To understand this seeming paradox, 'developmentalism' must be analysed and understood as a political and economic ideology of industrial society rather than as a set of universal theories and methods for addressing the many pressing problems facing poor countries.[11]

Developmentalism as modern mythology

As concept and as practice, development has become deeply ingrained in the 'culture', 'mythology' and day-to-day rhetoric of planners and politicians, and in the media and in the minds of billions of people around the world. The belief in economic man, in his intrinsic rationality and in the 'rituals' of systems analysis and planning that have been grounded on these assumptions is at the core of several widespread contemporary myths.

Nonetheless, the suggestion that these assumptions have anything to do with mythology is usually strongly resisted. It is countered with references to the 'truth' of the assumptions and the 'effectiveness' of their application. If this were unquestionably so, an alternative interpretation ought not to cause fear and defensiveness. However, it does, and the anxiety caused is only one more indication that what we are discussing is not an absolute 'truth', but received ideas. Seen as a belief system, 'developmentalism' could indeed benefit from a comparison with other world views.

Wallerstein has given an excellent illustration of ways modern myths emerge and of the functions they serve.

> Economic historians have built their work around organizing myths (more politely termed 'perspectives') which have informed, pervaded and underlain their work. An organizational myth is not a testable proposition. It is a tale, a metahistory, which seeks to provide a framework within which the structures, the cyclical patterns and the events of a given historical system may be interpreted. It can never be proven or refuted. It can only be propounded (and defended) as a heuristic device which explains more elegantly, coherently and convincingly than some alternative myth the historical system under observation and which leaves fewer puzzles unsolved or requires fewer ad hoc additional explanations to account for the empirical reality.[12]

Indeed, the mythology of developmentalism has become a normal part of our thinking. It guides our reflections and conditions our preferences. It has in Sartre's sense become 'a totalizing activity', which is the way in which he describes a dominant philosophy.

> Such a philosophy, Sartre suggests, is constructed under well-defined circum-
> stances for the purpose of giving expression to the general movement of society. A
> philosophy first of all is a particular way in which the 'rising' class becomes
> conscious of itself, but this consciousness must consistently strive to present itself
> as the totalization of existing knowledge. It effects the unification of everything
> that is known – of nature, of society and individuals, past, present and future, their
> metaphysical reflections on themselves, their fellows and their relationships to the
> infinite – following certain guiding schemata which express the attitudes and tech-
> niques of the rising class regarding its own period and the world.[13]

Sartre's view can be read as critique, but also as a prophesy of change to come when the 'locations' of power shift. This change will likely lead to the replacement of developmentalism by another social and political constella-tion, probably the disguised anonymous forces behind a globalizing market. This represents a major challenge. Knowledge must be mobilized to correct weaknesses and avoid blind support for a new mythology. To diminish some of the most obvious and dangerous threats, a profound transformation in thinking is required. For this transformation to occur, a new awareness about the rights of neglected and marginalized groups such as women, children, the elderly and minorities is necessary. These groups must be recognized as crucial partners in a fresh movement towards the betterment of the human condition.

Major biases in the ideology of development

In order to understand more about the nature of the debate on 'develop-ment', we need to examine the factors which may have contributed to the biases in the ideology of development. 'Development' has become a catch-all particularly within economics and political science. It is used to explain the 'nature' of historical processes especially in economic terms and to describe how and under what circumstances some of these processes might be mimicked or duplicated elsewhere.

The theoretical underpinnings in both the capitalist and the socialist approaches to 'development' derive from a positivist, natural science tradi-tion. This theoretical heritage has led to a focus on causative chains of reason-ing and a rejection of factors which do not easily lend themselves to such purposes. Development theorists have abstracted from reality what they judge essential for their explanations. Children, women, minorities and even

ordinary people in ordinary communities either do not matter in their calculations or do not fit into their models; consequently, they have been
neglected.

Preceding by half a century the warnings of Robert Chambers concerning
the juggernaut of 'normal science', Whitehead wrote in 1925 that:

> [the] dangers arising from [excessive professional specialization] are great.... The
> directive force of reason is weakened. They see this set of circumstances, or that set,
> but not both sets together. The task of coordination is left to those who lack either
> the force, or the character to succeed in some definite career. In short, the special-
> ized functions of the community are performed better and more progressively, but
> the generalized direction lacks vision. The progressiveness in detail only adds to
> the danger produced by the feebleness of coordination.[14]

Because of this theoretical and ideological selectiveness, the discussion of
development and of political economy in general has fallen into the trap
identified by Whitehead as the 'fallacy of misplaced concreteness', which he
described 'as neglecting the degree of abstraction involved when an actual
entity is considered merely so far as [the entity] exemplifies certain categories
of thought.'[15]

In his discussion of the work of Ricardo and the principles of economic
theory, Bagehot has described this fallacy in a way which well illustrates the
enormous danger of overabstraction for the sake of theoretical purity. He
writes that Ricardo 'thought he was considering actual human nature in its
actual circumstances, when he was really considering a fictitious nature in
fictitious circumstances.'[16]

Greatly influenced by these early warnings, Daly and Cobb have shown
how factors which should be at the very root of economic enquiry are
excluded from theories about reality in order not to disturb the assumptions
on which the interpretation of the nature of that reality is based.[17] This exclusion reflects two fallacies: first, the abstractions are formulated based on a
selective process, and, second, these abstractions are then used to stand in for
the total reality from which they have been abstracted. A fundamental
criticism of this sort of abstraction is presented in a concerned and prescient
statement by the Swiss economist de Sismondi, when he wrote in 1827 that:

> [the] new English economists are quite obscure and can be understood only with
> great effort because our mind is opposed to making the abstractions demanded of
> us. This repugnance is in itself a warning that we are turning away from the truth
> when, in moral science where everything is connected, we endeavour to isolate a
> principle and to see nothing but that principle... Humanity should be on guard
> against all generalizations of ideas that cause us to lose sight of the facts and above
> all against the error of identifying the public good with wealth, abstracted from the
> sufferings of the human beings who create it.[18]

One major and very damaging mistake dwarfs its many competitors within the already problem-ridden idea of 'development'. Made particularly in discussions of economics, it is the fundamental mistake which consists in confusing economic means with social goals, thereby treating people mainly as economic resources either as labourers or as consumers and viewing the production of goods and services as major 'development' aims. The basic assumption is that society is merely one more dependent variable in the working of an economic system. This is an absurd reversal of elementary logic, according to which the part is embedded in the whole. Here, on the contrary, society is wrongly viewed as being 'embedded' in economic behaviour.

Other factors which have contributed to the intellectual environment of development theory are rooted in a deep split in the Western world between what Snow has called the 'two cultures' of the sciences and the arts.[19]

Although Western in origin, this split has, together with the rapid globalization of science and technology, become the dominant international pattern. It is reflected in the difference between what are regarded as fundamental characteristics in projects of science, such as analysis and generally deductive explanation, and in projects of art, with their orientation towards interpretation and understanding. However, the myriad other differences which this split has generated in our interpretation of human reality are rarely examined. One of the most important can be described by reference to the two classical concepts of 'Gesellschaft' and 'Gemeinschaft' proposed by Toennies, the outstanding German observer of society. The former is usually identified with order and structure. According to this perspective, society is mainly conceived of in terms of the 'state'. The emphasis of 'Gemeinschaft' is more on community, human relationships and society as a living entity. However we may choose to define these two 'ideal' concepts, the former is componential and mechanical, while the latter tends to encompass relationships, participation and meaning.

Similar differences revolve around ambiguity and complexity and the relationships between the observer and the observed and between contents and boundaries, structures and processes.[20] The inspiration for many of these differences stems from the agonized rethinking taking place in quantum physics over the contrast between particle-like 'hard' phenomena and wavelike 'soft' phenomena. While economists and development theorists are preoccupied with what they regard as hard facts of great consequence for their explanatory efforts and theoretical constructions, theoretical physicists are increasingly regarding such a priori classifications as irrelevant and the biases to which they give rise as harmful. Similar conclusions were reached long ago through highly sophisticated reflection, especially in Hindu, Buddhist and Chinese philosophies. Dramatically new is the fact that such conclusions have received a strong boost from changes in the science of physics, which is at the very heart of the scientific tradition and which over the last 500 years has provided the principal models for the analysis of the nature of reality.

Factors in the exclusion of children in development theory

We are now better equipped to understand the main reasons for the neglect of children and women and other marginalized groups in the Western perception of development. Taking their cue from classical physics, economists and development theorists ignored or excluded from their abstracted models whatever was 'weak' or 'soft' and therefore of little consequence to their reasoning. Because developmentalism is essentially a political ideology, rather than the result of any theoretical project, there were further reasons to exclude groups which had no significance in terms of political and economic power. Indeed, the history of the idea of 'development' is the history not only of economic and political biases, but also of ethnocentric, male and age-related biases.

A story can illustrate the materialist and technological biases and the neglect of the dimensions of meaning and values in 'development'. It is a tale about the principles of an alternative economic theory which can help us gain a new perspective on the issue of labour and production that is so central in conventional development thinking. It is told by E.F. Schumacher in an article on Buddhist economics.

> There is universal agreement that the fundamental source of wealth is human labour.... The modern economist has been brought up to consider labour and work as little more than a necessary evil. From the point of view of the employer, it is in any case simply an item of cost, to be reduced to a minimum if it cannot be eliminated altogether, say, by automation. From the point of view of the workman, it is a 'disutility': to work is to make a sacrifice of one's leisure and comfort, and wages are a kind of compensation for the sacrifice. Hence the ideal from the point of view of the employer is to have output without employees, and the ideal from the point of view of the employee is to have income without employment.... [The] consequences of these attitudes both in theory and in practice are, of course, extremely far-reaching.[21]

As both employers and employees seem to share this view, we ought not to be astonished that unemployment in Western Europe, almost 30 years after the appearance of Schumacher's article, has climbed to an average of 10 per cent and continues to rise.

The Buddhist view is very different.

> [It] takes the function of work to be at least threefold: to give man a chance to utilize and develop his faculties, to enable him to overcome his egocentredness by joining with others in a common task, and to bring forth the goods and services needed for a becoming existence. Again the consequences flowing from this view are endless. To organize work in such a manner that it becomes meaningless, boring, stultifying or nerve-racking for the worker would be little short of criminal; it would indicate a greater concern with goods than with people, an evil lack of compassion and a soul-destroying degree of attachment to the most primitive side of the worldly existence. Equally, to strive for leisure as an alternative to work would be considered a complete misunderstanding of one of the basic truths of human existence, namely, that work and leisure are completely parts of the same living process and cannot be separated without destroying the joy of work and the bliss of leisure. From the Buddhist point of view, there are therefore two types of mechanization which must be clearly distinguished: one that enhances a man's skill and power and one that turns the work of man over to a mechanical slave, leaving man in a position of having to serve the slave. How to tell the one from the other?[22]

These and other views and values in a Buddhist theory of economics are very different from those of the economics of modern materialism. 'The Buddhist sees the essence of civilization not in the multiplication of wants, but in the purification of the human character.' This character is to a great extent formed by work. Therefore, work which is properly conducted blesses those who perform it and their products in equal measure. While the materialist is mainly interested in goods, the Buddhist is mainly interested in liberation.

For the modern economist, this is very difficult to understand. He is used to measuring the standard of living by the amount of annual consumption, assuming all the time that a person who consumes more is better off than is a person who consumes less. A Buddhist economist would consider this approach extremely irrational. The ownership and the consumption of goods are means to an end; an economist ought therefore to study how to attain ends with the minimum of resources.

Many factors have contributed to condition the nature, the biases and the surprising limitations of our knowledge about children and childhood. One, which is both a cause and a consequence, is a lack of the basic child-specific data which are required for a better theoretical understanding of the situation of children, as well as for policymaking and advocacy.

A factor which has had a significant influence on the nature and the location of the theoretical debate on children stems from the specific way in which the concept of child development has been used. Until recently, 'child development' mainly covered the physical, psychological and to some extent the social growth of the individual child. The theoretical debate has therefore been heavily focused on psychology, pædiatrics, early childhood care and education. In parallel there has been a theoretical neglect of children as children that is especially visible in macroeconomics, which has been the main discipline in the discourse on economic and social development. This has been harmful to children and their rights and, in the long run, to society.

Another factor behind the neglect of children is the belief that development is a process revolving around comprehensive progress. This ignores the fact that progress in one area may have negative repercussions in another. The following case highlighting the multiple effects and social costs of the expansion of irrigation in agriculture in Rajasthan in India illustrates this dilemma in a graphic way.

During recent decades the western parts of the large and beautiful waste-land of Rajasthan have been the site of one of the largest 'development' pro-jects ever undertaken in South Asia: the construction of the Indira Gandhi Canal, which was designed and financed jointly by the Indian Government and the World Bank. The canal has brought water for agricultural irrigation to the drylands where even camels sometimes must have worried about thirst and food security. Stony fields with scattered plots of sorghum and maize have given way to the impressive geometric shapes made by irrigation trenches and the vast crisscross of fields under cultivation and yielding two or three crops per year. Income has risen, although it has become more unevenly distributed. Income distribution now depends greatly on access to irrigation and the substantial transfers of land from the indebted to the better off farmers.

The pattern of labour has also changed dramatically, especially among women. It was always heavily skewed against them, but before the canal their main chores were performed in the house or near the homestead in close contact with other family members, especially with the other women. The switch to intensive agriculture and the constant work required on the high-yielding irrigated land have forced them to remain long hours away from their dwellings. The only way mothers and wives can manage all their other tasks, which have not been eliminated by the improved access to water, has been to rely heavily on their young daughters, while the boys have seen their chances of going to school improve because of the increase in family resources. This has resulted in a significant decline in the already unsatis-factory school attendance by girls and greater differences in workload, over-all life chances and well-being between girls and boys which are in favour of boys.

Corresponding lessons can be drawn from thousands of similar cases of technological change in many contexts. Heavier workloads among women in agriculture, industry or elsewhere are linked to drops in feeding frequency among infants and generally to greater risks to infant health. The ability of young girls to look after their smaller siblings is necessarily limited, and the care of smaller siblings by young girls erodes the quality of care of both the smaller siblings and the young girls. By reducing the educational opportunities for girls, technological change has also cut into the ability of young girls to mature into more fulfilled adults.

While food production is certainly important and needs to be strengthened, along with the overall viability of local farming, relevant and effective defensive strategies must also be introduced to offset and eventually to eliminate the higher costs of technological change to women, young girls and children. All the major economic and nutritional problems linked to change need to be addressed, not simply the problems in the area of food production.

Meanwhile, children have a right to be included as a focus in economic and political planning, and there can be no excuse, theoretical or otherwise, for excluding them from the consideration within economic and political development planning.

Human betterment and betterment for children

The recent international effort to shift the focus of the debate towards 'human development' represents a major attempt to solve some of the problems caused by the fact that economic growth is viewed as the only criterion, as well as the goal, of progress. However, real improvement cannot be achieved simply by introducing 'human development' as another subheading under 'development'. Instead, we must realize, as Kenneth Boulding suggested several decades ago, that the betterment of the human condition, in general and in context-specific terms, is the overriding criterion within which the contribution of all sectoral strategies, including the economic ones, should be considered.[23]

The effort to broaden the debate by incorporating goals and indicators covering survival, health, education and gender is a step in the right direction. This effort has largely emerged out of growing international concern with issues such as the environment, poverty and the situation of women and children. Two other important areas in which strategies are being rethought are structural adjustment and the transition from planned economies to market systems.[24]

Notable contributions towards changing the discourse from economic 'development' towards human betterment have sprung out of the persistent commitment to alternative development advocated, among others, by the Hammarskjold Foundation and by environmental groups and the new 'green' political movement. The work of UNICEF and more recently of the UN Development Programme, of the Save the Children movement, notably Save the Children-UK, and of the UN Research Institute for Social Development has led to significant inroads, as have individual scholars such as Hans Singer, Dudley Seers, Paolo Freire, Peter Berger, Kenneth Boulding, Barbara Ward, Keith Griffin, Mabub ul Huq, Richard Jolly, Frances Stewart, Giovanni

Andrea Cornia, David Korten and Norman Uphoff. Not least, Amartya Sen and his proposals for a social and economic development strategy based on a set of moral minima and intra- as well as inter-generational equity have played a key role in fostering a change in the groundrules of the debate.[25] A very healthy critical attitude has been maintained by students of anthropology and sociology such as, among many others, Kathleen Gough, Gerald Berreman, Scarlett Epstein, Haddad Assad, Sandra Wallman and Mary Racelis.

Even more important has been the work, combining deep understanding, compassion and a practical genius, undertaken by individuals and voluntary movements, some of which are mentioned in these essays, but most of which are only known and respected where they actually operate. They have been busy doing what others are discussing and have happily left renown and recognition for others to pursue. However, without their collective contributions the professional debaters would not be reminded of the risks when abstractions become divorced from reality and, one might add, from ethics. This is the dilemma which the now fashionable discussion on 'human development' ultimately is about.

Some fresh voices have provided new momentum to the process. In his recent book, *An Inquiry into Well-being and Destitution*, Partha Dasgupta has discussed the relationship between the conditions of children and the various household management and reproductive strategies of societies.[26]

From the somewhat different perspective of political science and economics, John O'Neill has attempted to remedy some of the prevalent theoretical neglect in his discussion of the 'missing child' in liberal theory.[27]

Neglected areas in the political and economic calculus have been identified by De Vylder in his discussion of the role of social capital and the need to rethink the issue of the investment needed for human and social development.[28] Such initiatives must be acknowledged, supported and carried on.

Economics as a discipline must also change. Economics must be deepened and broadened to take in all relevant dimensions in man's total 'reality room'. The idolization of the individual (male) and his supposed ability to make 'rational' choices, which are represented as intrinsic to economic and social actors, must be exposed for what it is: a myth. Likewise, economic analysis needs to cover everything which is valued in a society and not only what markets can immediately price through some means of exchange.

In *Essays on Persuasions*, John Maynard Keynes points to the dangers of the 'tunnel vision' of the majority of economists which has been created by their failure to place their calculations in a broader perspective. He criticizes their naive reliance on free market forces.[29] In his view, the invisible hand of classical economics can maximize output in the short run, but issues of kindness, justice and wisdom cannot be addressed by the market.

A new movement for the betterment of the human condition needs to build a solid foundation of knowledge and ethical insights. It must carefully consider the intellectual and political climate which developmentalism has created and assess what must be rejected and what can be retained. New visions need to be formulated. It should no longer be tolerated that theories about collective human behaviour – regardless of the personal or ideological preferences of the authors and their schools of thought – ignore the one-half of adult humankind who are women and more or less completely exclude the 35 per cent of the world's population that is represented by children. Only when these distortions are corrected will it be possible to repair some of the disastrous effects of the divorce from essential aspects of reality caused by the 'development' model, for which the words of General von Ludendorff may serve as an epitaph: 'If reality does not correspond to the map, follow the map.' We must redraw the map.

Notes and references

1. Nisbet (1969).
2. Friberg and Hettne (1985). See also Wallerstein (1994).
3. Wallerstein (1974), Wolf (1982) and Worsley (1984).
4. Friberg and Hettne (1985), page 220.
5. 'Chaos theory' has shown that systems can be deterministic without being predictable, that is, deducive. As indicators of the preferred assumptions of the authors, the more traditional use of the terms here is justified.
6. The exceptions are especially UNICEF and some international non-government organizations. Among the few exceptions among academics are P. Dasgupta, G. Kent and J. O'Neill. See Dasgupta (1993), Kent (1995) and O'Neill (1994).
7. World Bank (1993).
8. Esteva (1992), page 7.
9. Esteva (1992), pages 7ff.
10. Dahl and Hjort (1984).
11. An unfortunate gulf exists between, on the one hand, the view of 'development' in terms of ideology, culture, world outlook, lifestyle and the various combinations of underlying purposes, meanings and messages and, on the other, the monolithic view of development as unquestioned economic and technological progress. Until a dialogue between these two views can be established and taken seriously, there is little hope that the debate on development can be revitalized and achieve greater relevance for women, children, the poor, minorities and others among the excluded. For further discussions of these critical issues, see Wallman (1977), Said (1979), Brokensha, Warren and Werner (1980), Chambers (1983), Geertz (1983), Dahl and Hjort (1984), Apthorpe (1986) and Hobart (1993).
12. Wallerstein (1982).
13. Aseniero (1985), pages 53ff.
14. Whitehead (1925), page 200.
15. Whitehead (1929), page 11.
16. Bagehot (1953), page 157.
17. Daly and Cobb (1989).
18. de Sismondi (1827), cited in Daly and Cobb (1989), page 36.

19. Snow (1959).
20. Bohm and Peat (1987), Prigogine and Stengers (1984), Ploman (1986), Pylkanen (1989) and Waldrop (1993).
21. Schumacher (1968), pages 173ff.
22. Schumacher (1968), page 176.
23. Boulding (1985a).
24. UNICEF (1995c).
25. Sen (1987).
26. Dasgupta (1993).
27. O'Neill (1994).
28. De Vylder (1996). See also De Vylder (1995) and Banuri *et al* (1994).
29. See Hewlett (1993), page 51.

Essay 8: Recognizing the citizen child

In previous essays we have discussed the need for new approaches to the description of social reality and the identification of the problems facing children. We have also argued that we must rethink and reformulate the current paths to development and recognize children as both 'social actors in the making of policy [and] as the targets of policy'.[1] In order to lay a basis for finally recognizing the child as citizen we must consider the larger contexts of globalization and intergenerational perspectives as well as the more immediate political environments on the national and local levels. We must also consider the need for new partnerships for children and with children based on the conviction that the best interest of the child is in most cases also the best interest of the larger society.

Children, globalization and an intergenerational perspective

The world is witnessing accelerating technological, economic and cultural 'globalization'. This process has generally been viewed as an expansion. It can also be seen as a shrinking of the world and the world's resources. Shortages of major physical resources are being exacerbated by waste and environmentally destructive practices because of rapid industrialization and the explosion in consumerism. However, even the exploitative society is finally realizing, at least intellectually, that relatively soon we could be facing a dramatically dangerous situation. The globe itself is beginning to set the boundaries for what used to be 'open system' versions of globalization, in which the deficiencies or 'needs' of the centre countries could be satisfied through continued growth. Consequently, as the entire planet becomes the maximum operating field for major processes, the system is becoming a 'closed' one both theoretically and practically.

One important implication is that we must radically redefine the space and time dimensions in which planning and implementation for the betterment of the condition of children are considered. Generally, the time horizons applied in planning have been fixed according to the political interests of those in power, the availability of financial resources, the length of projects or other such external criteria. This must be replaced by a longer-term perspective which also recognizes the international and intergenerational nature of major child-related problems and the responsibilities of adult society.

It is no longer enough merely to project development aspirations in a linear fashion into the future. Instead, the path to an environment which can protect basic rights, promote the corresponding responsibilities and provide a combination of ample opportunities and fundamental security for the citizens of childhood must be sought and found. This requires that we dare to enter into a discussion on the nature of the good society with a view to identifying and promoting the acceptance of a few crucial characteristics, if not of some ideal or utopian society, at least of an acceptable or tolerable society which will be able to honour the universally negotiated principles of the Convention on the Rights of the Child. Such a discussion needs to pinpoint the goals and the requirements for a materially and economically viable society on the household level, the community level and the national and international levels. Similarly, there is a need to be precise about the minimum requirements for an acceptably competent society at these various levels, including access to a reasonable amount of power for children and their caregivers to create, monitor and maintain the conditions envisaged by the Convention on the Rights of the Child.

This means that our approaches to planning have to change. Planning must become an exercise in identifying that which is needed to reach or at least move closer to basic principles through a more long-term and phased strategy. However, during the effort to identify and move towards a good or better society, there must be constant vigilance against dogmatism. The risk of dogmatism is always present, but it is especially so when important questions of norms and values are involved. This risk is forcefully illustrated by nationalist, ethnic and religious fundamentalism, by bureaucratic socialism and most recently in the preaching of the theologians of the market, which they believe with equal fervour will compensate for most human shortcomings.

The recent discussion of human development is an attempt to create bridges between the prevalent mechanistic approach to development and a more normative one. In a contribution to philosophy and economics, Anand and Sen identify some of the consequences of the fact that 'development' claims to value 'human life itself'. They argue for comprehensive strategies which can make it possible for all individuals to enhance their capabilities.

This view requires that at least a reasonable level of equity can be attained. To Anand and Sen:

> distributional equity within and across generations constitutes the core principle of sustainable human development. The 'ethics of universalism of life' claims should therefore accord equal priority to equity today as against future generations.[2]

As Chen and Singh note, this concept of sustainable human development 'is clearly fundamental to strategies for children, who are the human bridges across generations'.[3]

Only recently have students of society, economy and culture tried to come to grips with some of the consequences of the dramatic shifts in the time-space dimension that have been generated by the globalization of knowledge, of technology and of the organization of economic transactions and in the transmission of cultural images and lifestyles throughout the world.[4] These changes have created rapidly expanding social spaces in which and through which people interact over global distances and share and communicate through globally dispersed constellations of knowledge, values and aspirations. This has also had an effect on children and their situations, our perceptions of them and children's perceptions of themselves.

What then is 'global' about globalization? Despite the shrinking world, we do not live on a global level, but always in some localized context such as the village of Tokha in the Kathmandu Valley or the Upper East Side of Manhattan. What may be global in both these places is the growing probability that in managing our lives we will draw on resources – physical, social or mental – that come from somewhere else on planet Earth. These resources are not global per se. Thus, what is global cannot be found in a specific entity.

We must therefore search for the 'global' in the sphere of relationships. Something is global because it is generated and maintained through relationships which connect, combine and often also direct the use of technological, social and intellectual resources which come from somewhere else on planet Earth. We need to remind ourselves that, precisely when global changes of this sort are occurring, we must direct our energies into scrutinizing the nature of our theoretical assumptions – hidden or explicit – and alter not only our maps, but also our tools for orientation and exploration.[5]

The issue is not so much that the world is becoming one, but that it is becoming many, and these many worlds increasingly operate on a global scale and relate to each other in new and quickly changing ways. Access to technology, transportation, communication and information generates a series of 'worlds' or 'social fields' which are smaller or larger, accessible or inaccessible and manageable or difficult to manage depending on one's relative ability to control some of the factors behind them.

Children and childhood are rarely discussed within these larger contexts. UNICEF's efforts to initiate a debate on economic adjustment 'with a human face' that would expose the often damaging consequences for children of macroeconomic strategies and fiscal policies has in many ways been an exception. However, if we want to include children in our debate on development and betterment, it is necessary to examine their situation from these perspectives as well. The discussion on adjustment established the linkages between global economic policy decisions and negative outcomes for children. It is important to establish similar multi-level linkages if we wish to discuss responsibilities and accountability in development. A story can illustrate this need more aptly than a prolonged theoretical discussion.

The situation of many children in the Himalayan hills today can help us understand what the globalization of values, aspirations and behaviour can mean for children. Consumerism and the sex trade offer striking examples of some of the economic and social dimensions of pervasive globalization. In some areas of South Asia and South East Asia the income-generating potential of prostitution has few, if any, rivals at the village level. The sex trade provides the possibility of a quantum leap in earnings that one would otherwise find only in a socioeconomic environment in which there are adequate education, small-scale industries, public services and opportunities for salaried employment.

The new wealth obtained from the sex market can sustain radically new lifestyles. This is especially so in the case of the (mostly male) parasites who live off the sex workers, and spend their time leisurely and still have access to many times the resources available to hard-working agricultural labourers. The easy income rapidly weakens one of the few safety nets available to the poor: collective solidarity and the values placed on group work. Without these supports, the possibilities of earning a living in the hills are severely hampered.

The brutalization of the relationships within the families from which women and girls are trafficked greatly aggravates gender disparity. Girl children and women, whose social and economic position is already weaker than that of men, have become the targets of the brutality and the main victims of the sex trade.

In an overview of prostitution and the trafficking of Nepalese women and girls to India, O'Dea asks who the clients are.[6] She finds that, like the merchants of the sex trade, they come from all over India and vary by origin and socioeconomic status. Furthermore, there are around 300000 Nepalese migrating seasonally to India, and another 150000 hold down army and security jobs. Many are single, while others are separated from their wives and children. Not all buy sex. However, of those who do, many like to be with their own people, who share the same background and language.

Besides the Nepalese, there are also tourists from the region and from around the world. Among these, there is an exclusive 'club' of men from countries in the Middle East who are willing to pay high prices for virgins and minors. To satisfy this demand it has been reported that special auctions have been held to sell off minor girls. The rise in the number of child prostitutes – among whom most of the girls for auction are found – is also for this reason a growing concern.

Like the buyers and the sex merchants, the business managers in the sex trade come from various socioeconomic backgrounds and hold varying amounts of power. The 'controllers', who are directly involved with the girls, are unscrupulous merchants who own brothels, hotels and restaurants; the madams handle the hiring and trafficking and run the brothels, and the pimps and strongmen, who sometimes torture and rape, even gang rape, the young girls, are willing to withhold food and water until the girls are 'broken in'. The young girls are the victims in a process of 'culturally designed moral debasement and physical battering'. The controllers make 'women and children undergo a slow or rapid metamorphosis from respectable persons with dignity and freedom to sellers of sex and slavery'.[7]

Sadly, the world is moving into the Himalayan hills of Nepal in company with the underworld, bringing new aspirations, images and resources, but also sexual diseases transmitted by returnees – escaped, rescued or retired – HIV and AIDS and, worse, a new generation of violated children, robbed of their childhood and their human rights and traumatized for life.

Other forces – personal and impersonal – are working together directly or indirectly to maintain a situation which eventually transforms young girls into commodities of exchange in a regional and global market of gender exploitation and sexual violence. Among these forces are national, regional and global inequities which generate poverty and the consumer urges communicated by the media, tourism and the market globalization that transplants images of purpose and meaning from elsewhere. The abuse of girls in the Himalayan hills of Nepal is a horrifying illustration of some of the negative consequences for children of the expansion of global market forces.

The lessons to be drawn are clear. Poverty, widening socioeconomic imbalances, expanding contacts with the outside world and the erosion of values are emerging hand in hand with a breakdown in traditional economic structures and a loss in social cohesion. The risks which these changes generate need to be identified and offset by education, the spread of awareness and the promotion of appropriate and effective economic policies, in combination with the more intense protection of human rights and the rights of the child.

The political environment of children

In most cultural traditions it has been common to regard the child as property. The Roman law of *pater potestas* allotted the authority over the life and death of the child to the father. In traditions in which the family is extended through formalized kinship relationships to larger units, the child may be described as belonging to the community. Following the emergence of the nation-state, children and parents were sometimes viewed as the property of the state, and consequently childhood became a tool to be manipulated by the state for its own purposes. In contrast, the rapid social fragmentation, the commercialization of human affiliations and the radical transformation in lifestyles that have coincided with industrialization have so changed society that in some countries even divorce by children from their parents can be legally contemplated.

To understand the political realities of children, one needs to look at children as political actors and examine carefully the nature of the political environment surrounding children and the political processes on all levels, from the immediate localities in which the children live to the national and international arenas which affect their lives.

The single most important factor in the political situation of children and one which must be given serious attention is children's lack of power. Not only are children dependent, but they don't have any political leverage either.

Democracy, however it may be defined, is expanding. At least in theory there has been an accompanying rise in the importance of voters and a parallel inflation in the attention which politicians are giving to potential groups of voters. Since the eligibility to vote is associated with the age of maturity, which is socially defined, children are not part of an attractive pool of potential voters to be courted. In the competition for resources, they therefore often lose out to other groups. This is negatively affecting resource allocations for child-related causes, despite frequently intense lobbying by parents and child rights organizations.

It is thus a crucial challenge for the democratic system to find ways to recognize, respect and respond to a child population which, for many valid reasons, can neither articulate nor defend many of its own fundamental interests and, for equally valid reasons, cannot be granted the voting rights or other political powers of their fellow citizens. Child issues must be moved closer to the centre of politics and policymaking. The urgency of this stems from the fact that changes in the technological, economic, social and cultural environments of children in all parts of the world are drastically transforming the political environment of children and childhood. In poor and rich countries alike, childhood is eroding from neglect. Families are not holding together; schools do not teach; politics invites cynicism; companies exploit and environments are being polluted. All over the world fewer and fewer people are becoming active citizens, and more and more are becoming anonymous members of the masses. The distance between governments and communities has increased. Governments have grown larger and more impersonal. Communities have been ground small between a non-participatory industrial culture and eroding traditional and natural environments.

The basic human right to live and grow and to be recognized and respected has become a casualty, not an achievement. This is not only dangerous, since isolation and marginalization breed many of society's ills, but it is also unrealistic and ineffective and therefore bad politics.

Whatever the nature of the problems of betterment that we face, the most basic among them must ultimately be solved by people, and 'people' includes children. Numerous cases illustrate what can be achieved and sustained when communities and voluntary organizations apply their energies, knowledge, skills, leadership and managerial capacity.[8]

To plead for a change in emphasis is not to argue for the neglect of humanitarian welfare or physical infrastructure or for growth in material terms. It is a plea to correct the 'loud' distortions which have crept in because of serious institutional decline. It is a call to return not only to the roots of problems, but also to the level where the action is: the small rural community, the tribal village and the urban slum. Today, that community, that village and that slum are diminished, fragmented, unorganized, not fully informed. While there are many forums for discussion and supportive action, these can never take the place of community solidarity and group action mediated by non-government organizations and supported by informed and committed government employees working effectively together.

It is fairly clear from the ongoing debate on the relative role of the state and the market in the development process that both are essential, but that neither can be the prime mover. The role of the state needs to be reoriented and made more effective, not weakened or eliminated, in support of a revamped development strategy. Such discipline and efficiency as the market can bring to bear must be reinforced by urgent affirmative action to assure the survival and security of the poor. The poor themselves must be enabled to become the engine of change. The political, legal and administrative systems ought to provide an environment which enables the poor to organize themselves with the help of voluntary agencies, professional expertise and the support – or at the very least the acquiescence – of government.

Towards a partnership approach

Without a revitalized and resourceful state and the political commitment of elected representatives and government, human development goals like health for all, education for all and the eradication of discrimination against women and girls will remain utopian. Such efforts at revitalization must be combined with meaningful policies for the decentralization of planning and decision-making to the levels where the problems exist and where the people live who face the problems. To achieve this the democratic transfer of real power to communities through a functioning representative system of local governance is crucial. A truly representative local government is needed to assist the marginalized and the excluded, so that they can organize and become informed and so that they can plan and manage socioeconomic pro-grammes which are relevant to them and their children. Real power and resources must devolve to local governments. Only in this way can these governments transform themselves into democratic institutions, raise cost-effectiveness and strengthen accountability. In the process, it should also be possible to achieve tremendous savings if and when the need for inadequate and ineffective bureaucratic structures is reduced. Voluntary non-govern-ment organizations with a local presence and a credible track record will have a central role to play in mediating and supporting a genuine com-munity, government and professional partnership by mobilizing resources, raising awareness and carrying out training.

In these efforts we need to respond to the spectrum of the basic needs of all, as distinct from the special wants of some, if we are to assure that even one of those needs is met in a sustainable fashion. In other words, the right of the child to betterment means the right of the child to a political and socio-economic system which is determined to work energetically for it.

Urie Bronfenbrenner has made important proposals in this regard which constitute, paraphrasing Amartya Sen, a moral minimum for child-related development.

> The effective functioning of child-rearing processes in the family and other child settings requires public policies and practices that provide place, time, stability, status, recognition, belief systems, customs and actions in support of child-rearing activities not only on the part of parents, caregivers, teachers and other profes-sional personnel, but also relatives, friends, neighbours, co-workers, communities and major economic, social and political institutions of the entire society.[9]

In such a strategy, the needs, rights and space of children must be recognized according to the principle of the child not as a noble cause for charitable action, but as a worthy citizen, a principle adapted to the various phases of childhood, but no less meaningful because of the dependency of children and their overall status as a minority in a dominantly adult society.

A concrete story will help us realize the qualitative, ethical and intellectual ingredients of a partnership approach. It is a brief story about some 20 years of work by two of the most gifted and professionally respected Indian medical doctors, Mabelle Arole and Rajanikant Arole, who, as the recipients of the prestigious Asian 'Nobel' Prize, the Malagsay Award, cannot be labelled simply as romantic bush doctors.

All the elements of a partnership approach are contained in the story: the need for committed and professionally competent initiators, inspirers and facilitators, the partnership between concerned professionals and the community, supportive voluntary organizations and a reasonably positive official structure. The story therefore satisfies our expectations. However, the really interesting part is represented by the surprises experienced by all the participants involved.

It began when the two Aroles decided that improving health especially among children would be the only worthwhile way they could apply their skills. Despite the scepticism of all their colleagues, they chose to travel to Jamkhed in the State of Maharashtra, one of the most isolated and destitute places on the Indian subcontinent and, indeed, on earth. The situation is well described by a woman who became one of their teachers. Her name was Lalanbai Kadam. She said the following to the two medical technologists.

> I am a Dalit widow. I used to think that I was nobody. I lived in constant fear because I was treated worse than an animal.... My son died when he was less than 3 years old, and I was blamed for it and sent away by my husband. My parents made me marry an old man who had tuberculosis, and he also died. I returned to the village in shame. I lived in darkness. To support myself I swept and cleaned the village and did hard manual labour and received a pittance. Even dogs were welcome in the houses, but I, as a Harijan, was not. Then along with other women, we decided not to accept this any more.[10]

Thanks to people like Lalanbai Kadam and the Aroles, many hundreds of thousands of marginalized men, women and children in Maharashtra realized the potential within themselves to improve their living conditions and their health. It is fashionable in this instance to use the word 'empowerment', one of the most pleasing misnomers of the elite. The 'power' to improve the situation is already there; the challenge lies in discovering the way to allow that power to come forth.

Within less than two decades, the infant mortality rate – a major indicator of health – had been reduced from 175 to 18 per 1 000 live births, and the birth rate had fallen from over 40 per 1 000 to 17. It took a century to achieve the same results in Europe and North America. How did this happen? The short answer is that two highly educated persons decided that their education had just begun and that they had to train themselves to listen in order to make their professional competence meaningful and useful.

The long answer is also very much worth giving. Here, it is excerpted from the Aroles' own summary. It started as a well-intentioned effort to provide curative services especially for suffering children. In the parlance of these essays, it was a charitable undertaking. It soon became evident to the Aroles that poor people are not interested in health. They are interested in relief from unbearable pain. Other illnesses are mere irritations. The people said:

> We need water. We need jobs so that we can buy food to kill the hunger pangs, and then we will not have to migrate to cut sugar cane. You ask us to wash our hands. Where is the water? Do you know the cost of soap?[11]

In response, the Aroles decided to live on the same average income as the villagers, and to learn the real cost of soap. They soon found out that it would take them two days of hard work to buy a tiny bar of soap. The Aroles report:

> It was we who had to change first.... How can we share scientific information in a meaningful way unless we understand [their] problems? ... Water needed to flush a toilet [cost] more than a two months' wage.... The poor people taught us how they cope with the situation, born out of experience. Their felt needs of food and water were more important than our health interventions.[12]

The Aroles set aside their interest in the health care which they were trained to provide and concentrated on providing water. However, the low-caste and the outcast people were worried. How would they get access to water if it was found in the part of the village where 'the high and mighty' lived? The Aroles consulted their conscience and got the water diviner to agree that he would only report the sources of water he found in the low-caste areas. If the water sources had been located in the high-caste areas, the water would have been out of reach for the lower castes and the untouchables.

Thanks to the wise geo-political guidance of the small health team, all 150 tubewells were drilled in the areas shunned by the powerful. But since water was in high demand, everyone, whether rich or poor, Brahmin or outcast, flocked there. Contacts were made over seemingly insurmountable social and cultural barriers.

As another benefit of this situation, the two outsiders were finally trusted by the poor. At first, they had tried to work with the community leaders. They realized that the approach was not the right one. Improvement, also for children, required the participation of the entire community, fragmented and divided as it was. Much of the starvation and undernutrition were caused by social attitudes towards women and children. To change these the reality that religion, caste and politics divided both rich and poor people had to be faced.[13]

To create an understanding of the shared nature of problems across century-old lines of division, the two promising medical scientists, neither of them really in Olympic form, started volleyball games in a number of villages. After a game, where individuals could shine regardless of their background or status, both onlookers and players would stand around and talk. The game soon became the meeting place where problems in the village and in the development of the community were discussed.[14]

The story goes on. For example, women were encouraged to enter into discussions with government officials and the well-dressed employees of banks. The results in terms of strengthened confidence and increased opportunities for self-employment and an accompanying investment in the welfare of the children of the women were dramatic.

The concluding statement of the Aroles identifies more clearly than any theoretical discourse what betterment for children and women should be about.

> People are the key actors in health and human development. Poor people have coping mechanisms based on collective experience and wisdom. It is important to recognize this and enhance their skills and knowledge so as to increase their choices. Addressing economic poverty and building large infrastructures alone will not lead to [better conditions for children. Betterment] depends on individual and community action. The knowledge to acquire and maintain this is a human right. Professionals need to demystify their knowledge. It should be shared in such a way that people can assess, analyse and make the right choices. The knowledge should liberate us and not intimidate us. It should lead to building self-esteem and confidence in oneself and in others.[15]

In the words of a woman with many children in the dryland of Jamkhed:

> People are like wick lamps: simple, inexpensive and unattractive. But unlike the chandeliers (which professionals are), the wick lamp has a tremendous energy. It is capable of lighting another lamp and another and another ... to cover the whole planet.[16]

In the end, the people of Jamkhed decided to abolish the caste system in their area. This represented the culmination of their efforts to establish a community spirit built on decency and solidarity and with the political goal of reducing barriers and optimizing opportunities for all. In the longer run, this proved to be especially important for the children, who could expand their contacts, their experiences and their supportive social networks.

Partnerships among disciplines

The same principle of partnership should be applied to the field of knowledge so as to offset the limiting and distorting effects of the sectoralization which still prevails in the planning and implementation of betterment strategies, including those for children.

In education, for example, much effort has gone into the design of infra-

structure and the collection of enrolment statistics, while relatively little attention has been paid to making education relevant and teaching exciting. This
has led to the expansion of educational facilities, but only rarely to improvements in the quality and effectiveness of education. This is particularly noticeable in the struggle to improve education among girls. Nonetheless, when
schools are not functioning properly because there are no materials or because
the teachers are not there, both boys and girls suffer. Therefore, rather than
looking for technological fixes or attractive incentives to boost the enrolment
of girls, one ought to pay attention to other, more fundamental needs.

This should not imply that there are no special measures, whether social,
technical or economic, which can make a positive contribution to the
enrolment, retention and learning achievements of girls. Indeed, even the
much-discussed Bangladesh Rural Advancement Committee (BRAC) has
been successful in fostering the education of girls not because it has come up
with a magic formula but because the primary education offered has had the
proper mix of the basics: an interesting, uncluttered curriculum, flexible
school schedules, motivated teachers, supervision and community participation. BRAC and other successful education movements have acted on the
insight that being innovative amounts to doing the obvious. This is sometimes forgotten in expensive and prestigious conferences about innovative
approaches, which often serve as an escape from and an excuse for avoiding
the tedious, less glamorous, day-to-day effort.

To BRAC it was obvious that the teacher had a key role. One of the most
serious failures in education systems is precisely the weakness in the support
systems for teachers. However, the motivation and success of teachers do not
reside merely in better pay and better working conditions, but mainly in
offering them proper support and encouragement and more opportunities
for them to learn, expand their knowledge, cooperate with each other, be
respected and achieve the confidence to do their job as best as they can.[17]

To improve education among girls, we need to know why more girls are
not participating and take the steps necessary to remedy this. We will not
find this information in any macrostudies on education systems. The national
policy level is no doubt important, but the major problems are found among
the schools, where the girl child does or does not enrol, where she continues
school or drops out, and where she learns something to enable her to become
more in control over her own life or not. We must therefore examine the various forces which act at the community level and chalk out the specific steps
which need to be taken by the community, by teachers, by parents and by
local, regional and central governments to facilitate basic education for the
vast majority of girls.

This requires a thorough understanding of how the local community functions and how decisions are taken. Is it only the parents who decide whether
a girl goes to school? If so, what is it that persuades them to send their girl to

school? Their own literacy? Or are the decisive factors to be found in the overall cultural and social climate of the community? How does the traditional division of labour influence the educational opportunities for girls? What role does poverty play? If a 'poor' girl drops out of a 'bad' school, is poverty to blame or is the school to blame? Can a reasonable, flexible, accessible and interesting learning environment offset even the worst poverty and deprivation? Does poverty stifle education? Can education overcome poverty?

We must have the courage to turn the conventional wisdom on its head. Too little thought and too little effort have been directed toward weighing the scales in favour of education. Indeed, basic education, especially for girls, is one of our best trump cards for real and sustainable development not only for girls and women, but also for the community and for society at large.[18] The BRAC experience in Bangladesh and many experiences in Bhutan, Brazil, Colombia, India, Sri Lanka, Tanzania and elsewhere indicate that this is possible. The debate on betterment for children needs to learn from them.

In child health care, a major part of the effort, especially within UNICEF, has been focused on technology. Technological advances have no doubt contributed to the betterment of children's health and to an often dramatic and rapid reduction in infant and child mortality rates in most countries. However, important techniques and effective equipment are often produced and promoted by medical establishments and pharmaceutical companies which are closely allied with elite groups of individuals who have little understanding of, or interest in, ordinary people and their concerns.

The technology bias persists despite the fact that poor health and disease all too often are closely associated with social and cultural factors. The connection between diarrhoea and poverty provides a striking illustration. It is no secret that those who die of diarrhoea are mainly the poor who lack education and who have little or no access to clean water or sanitation. Diarrhoea is in fact the disease of social deprivation and the affliction of those most in need. Any effective and sustainable solution is therefore inseparable from the fight against poverty, unemployment, ignorance and the many other disparities which divide our communities.

Since the development of oral rehydration therapy in Calcutta and Dhaka, the use of this life-saving technique has spread around the world. However, in the quest for rapid and effective medical solutions, the importance of food, feeding and suitable childcare has been overshadowed; the importance of proper nutrition must be communicated by all health workers to communities and the families caring for the child with diarrhoea.

There are close linkages between social and environmental deficiencies and the biological 'rebellion' which diarrhoea represents. Because of this, a major challenge today is behavioural change. While we have found temporarily workable answers to diarrhoea in the form of safe water and sanitation through oral rehydration therapy, sound feeding practices and effective antibiotics, the management of diarrhoea at home and within the community remains obstructed by old misconceptions and inappropriate practices on the part of professionals and the public.

One urgent behavioural change relates to breastfeeding, which, in combination with immunization, attention to personal hygiene, improved community sanitation and the introduction of appropriate nutrient-rich weaning foods, will improve the health and nutritional status of the child and help to turn the wheel of death caused by diarrhoea and malnutrition into a wheel of life. Furthermore, effective basic education, a women-centred betterment to combat the evils of gender-inequality, and the strengthening of the capabilities and the participation of communities are imperative if goals in child health and in health for all are to be achieved.

Much of the debate on development focuses on the need to protect the physical environment. In fact, few conditions capture more readily the human dimension of the concern for the environment than does diarrhoea. Diarrhoea is essentially a disease of the environment, and we can catch the attention of political and social leaders by clearly establishing this linkage and the need to deal with it. Indeed, monitoring chronic diarrhoea among children could be an effective way of dramatizing the state of the environment. Unhealthy settlement patterns, the scarcity of clean drinking water and the unhygienic disposal of human and other waste materials are all causes of diarrhoea. The immediate requirements of ordinary people in poor countries for the provision of safe water, effective sanitary measures and functioning day-to-day life support systems are crucial for an environmentally sound development and must, finally, be upgraded to the level of a major global responsibility.

The timing and spacing of the birth of children in families, the number of children in families, overall population growth and mounting urbanization are also important causative factors in diarrhoea. The larger the family, the more its efforts to protect and improve the lives of its members will be impeded by high costs, lack of time and deficient care. Concern for the situation of individual poor families should be the starting point for a more effective advocacy of small family size. Exponential population growth and global forecasts of additional billions of people on earth may worry demographers and politicians, but they have little relevance at the level of families and households, where the root causes of the reproductive explosion must be found. Even in cases in which, for various reasons, a greater number of offspring in a family is considered an asset, awareness can be created – must be created – that the overcrowding of families and households will also and necessarily crowd out the ambitions of the same families to provide a decent and healthy livelihood not only for the children, but also for the adults.

Again, we must recognize that the solution of macro-problems must include the level of the micro-units where ultimately the critical decisions will be made. Therefore, the eradication of diarrhoea and other major killers of children that stimulate parents to maintain high rates of reproduction is, together with the reduction of poverty, at least over a sufficient time span, also an effective strategy for dealing with the problem of runaway population growth.

Once we have understood all these linkages, we will also understand that in the end a major goal of human betterment must be to promote not only health for the child, but a healthy society and a healthy culture for all children.

On children's rights as a blueprint for betterment

The perception that the 'suffering of children' is unjust and therefore constitutes a breach of the 'rights' of children to a decent life has been a facet of the movement to protect and enhance the situation of children from the start, although the early articulations of the rights were tentative and vague. The efforts to include concern for children in development planning that began in earnest in the 1960s may actually be seen as an attempt to use development strategies to achieve goals related to the rights of children.

International political and legal negotiations intensified during the 1980s. This resulted in the adoption of the Convention on the Rights of the Child. The Convention has helped create a potentially new political situation in favour of children. It aims to alter perceptions about children and childhood and to foster the promotion of fundamental universal values in a world of far-reaching cultural, social, economic and political diversity. Although drafted and adopted primarily for normative and legal purposes, the Convention nonetheless represents a breakthrough in policymaking for the betterment for children. It indicates areas in which rights exist and should be protected and identifies goals and priorities for short- and long-term betterment strategies. Thus, the Convention stresses the continuum between child rights and child betterment. Both are related and ought eventually to be united by the need to respect, protect and fulfil the rights of all children and to honour the consequent claims on resources, opportunities and social participation for children. In many cases the Convention advocates major changes in common assumptions and prevalent practices. It therefore provides an important point of departure for a revitalized international debate on childhood and betterment for children generally.

Much of the discussion of child rights by human rights experts has centred around the goals of respecting, protecting and fulfilling the articles of the Convention. To 'respect' child rights implies strengthened advocacy for children. To 'protect' them requires, in addition, a decisive involvement of the state, the legal system and law enforcement agencies. To 'fulfil' the articles of the Convention adds the duty to undertake the political, economic and social initiatives necessary to achieve a meaningful betterment of the conditions of childhood, as well as for the individual child, with due recognition of age differences, dependency on adults and to some extent acceptable cultural variations.

The articles of the Convention can be divided into five major clusters covering the right of children to respect and identity,[19] basic needs for survival,[20] protection from war, abuse, exploitation, abandonment and other difficult circumstances,[21] a generally caring society[22] and an enabling environment. In addition to its focus on the specific rights of children, the Convention also embraces broad issues such as the obligation of the state to allocate critical resources for children in terms of finances, expertise and administrative arrangements. It calls for the establishment of universal primary education and special efforts in education to redress inequities and distortions related to gender. It identifies the obligations to be met through international official development assistance and supports more balanced opportunities for poor countries in the organization of international trade. It outlines the efforts to be undertaken to reduce poverty and increase the participation of local communities. It also emphasizes that governance and management must be improved.[23]

Thus, the Convention is clearly not limited to a mere listing of rights. Nonetheless, further work is needed to build the bases for translating the Convention into reality. To move in that direction, we must be prepared to advocate changes of a wider social, cultural, economic and political nature, so as to create favourable conditions and opportunities in the environments surrounding children. We must develop communications and information strategies to reorient individual and community values as well as public policies, so that they truly include children and childhood in theory and in practice.

Since the promulgation of the Convention, discussions about it have concentrated mainly on legal analyses and interpretations of the various articles, on the efforts to monitor compliance and on the advocacy of child rights.[24] Some attention has also been devoted to the fiscal and budgetary implications of the implementation of the Convention.[25] Comparatively less attention has been given to the identification of priorities in information gathering, research and practical work at various levels of society to create the conditions necessary to implement the Convention. Today, a major challenge before those working to make the Convention a reality is therefore the identification of politically and economically feasible goals and the promotion of the theoretically valid and ethically sound changes required at various levels of society.

The best interests of the child and the best interests of society

Some of the major obstacles to the betterment of children are grounded in a misunderstanding of the significance of childhood, the absence of a proper recognition of the obligations placed on children collectively by adult society, deficiencies in the rights of citizenship of children and a corresponding disregard of the other rights of children. There is a damaging theoretical neglect of children, especially in economic analyses, a failure to adopt a truly intergenerational perspective and a lack of a reasonable participation of children in civic affairs. Other obstacles in the way of a more thorough acceptance of the Convention on the Rights of the Child are due to actual or perceived contradictions between the best interests of adult society and the best interests of the child.

Many of the worst abuses of children take place within the family or are perpetrated by adults in the child's local environment. In situations of poverty and in highly labour-intensive economies, children are regarded as labourers and providers of additional income. In other situations, their contribution to society and to the state is not expected to begin to materialize until they are nearly adults. This places children and childhood in competitive situations in terms of the allocation of financial resources. The perception that children are mainly beneficiaries of the support of parents and society, together with children's lack of power generally, places them in a weak position.

It is clearly important and necessary to move away from the tendency to look at the problem as 'children versus society' and move towards a view focusing on children and society. To do this, we need to turn the debate around and envision betterment for children not only as the establishment of rights for children, but also as the establishment of the duties of society. Thus, it is important to demonstrate that it is an obligation for adult society to promote the rights of children. However, it is also helpful to show that this actually represents an opportunity for society. Indeed, many of society's more utilitarian and achievement-oriented interests in children would be well served by supporting the ethical principles of the rights of the child. If such linkages between the rights of the child and the interest of society can be convincingly demonstrated, the grounds for influencing policies can be dramatically strengthened. In attempting to promote a pro-child political agenda, it is therefore useful to locate and analyse children's rights and devise strategies to promote them within the larger context of the surrounding society.

To illustrate what this might mean, we now look at some of the major components of the Convention not only from the perspective of the child, but from the perspective of the surrounding society as well. This will also help us to estimate the cost to society of not supporting a child-centred policy.

Recognition and respect

Recognition and respect must be accorded to the child in the same way as they are, or at least ought to be, accorded to all citizens. We do not need volumes of research or complicated analyses to realize the importance of this for the creation of a positive identity and of self-respect in the child, leading to a confident, creative and resourceful adult. The value of this to society is as obvious as the cost of a non-confident, non-creative, impoverished individual. Experience with child abuse, exploitative child labour and gender discrimination is the surest indicator that the best interests of the child and the best interests of society are badly served by not protecting the rights of children.

Furthermore, recognition and respect require sufficient individual and social space for children and opportunities for play, exploration and participation and for the unfolding of potential and growth. These constitute essential bridges between childhood and the adult world. For society, these bridges represent extremely rich sources of creativity and human development. When they are neglected, isolation, withdrawal and loss of growth and self-worth combine to damage children and the wider society alike.

Protection and support

Protection and support cannot be provided for the child without the meaningful efforts of parents, family, caregivers and the institutions of childhood. Lacking physical, psychological and social health, the child cannot preserve its resourcefulness, dignity and well-being. The cost of deficiencies in this regard will be dramatic. For the child, the deficiencies will cause unnecessary suffering. For society, they will lead to a drain on social resources and a significant reduction of the contribution of children to the reproduction and maintenance of society. High infant mortality rates, poverty, drug abuse, child labour and the absence of childhood institutions or lack of participation in them are some of the tragic costs.

Preparation for a rewarding life

The acquisition of appropriate and adequate technical, organizational, social and cultural skills by the child is essential both for the child and for the surrounding society. This is the basis for a progressively rewarding contribution to the creation and management of a fruitful life based on competent activities and accumulated experience which benefit both the child and society. Lacking this basis, the child will be more or less permanently disadvantaged. Low school enrolment rates, illiteracy, discrimination against girls, street children, slum settlements and many other problems show us what can happen to children and to society at large if this is neglected.

Resources

Children have a right to resources for survival, health and protection and resources for the acquisition of knowledge and skills. Financial, informational and political resources are required for children and caregivers. One of the most neglected resources is access to adequate information, so that one can understand and evaluate the child's situation from the perspective of the child and from the perspective of the rest of society. Deficiencies in the allocation of financial and informational resources will inevitably lead to a reduction in the physical, intellectual and social growth of the child and ultimately of the child's potential to contribute to society.

An exercise of this kind reveals the striking similarities among development goals (which also imply rights) from the outlook of the child and from the perspective of society. Likewise, there is a close affinity between the consequences and the costs for society on the one hand and the lack of protection for the rights of children on the other.

A careful comparison between the two sets of perceptions, society's and the child's, represents a precious opportunity to identify ways to strengthen advocacy and political action. Instead of viewing children's rights and society's obligations mainly as a pair of opposites, such a comparison allows us to understand the child more clearly and to look at the obligations of adults and of society not as a burden to be reluctantly accepted, but as something good, desirable and eventually very rewarding. The rights of the child are not only beneficial to the child. The respect for, and protection and fulfilment of, these rights by the child's society also represent in a very real sense the best interests of that society.

Immediate challenges

Thus far, our discussion of ways to achieve recognition of children as citizens in their own right has remained on the rather general level of principles and goals. This is necessary. But we must also have the courage to ask the simple questions: what are some possible first steps? who can do what now? In trying to respond to these questions, we need to sharpen our capacity to listen so that we do not perceive children as small adults searching for their own version of an adult agenda. No matter which practical steps we recommend or promote, we must begin with the understanding that children are important in their own right, and we must relate, negotiate and work with them in the specific contexts within which their age and individuality (and ours) are found. While the general goals of the Convention should be accepted as the overall context for action, we have the right and the obligation to identify and select pragmatic first steps in areas where a possibility for such action exists or can be fostered. These steps are also needed to initiate and facilitate the longer journey toward the full implementation of the rights of the child.

No theory about society, politics or economy can be credible if the 40 per cent of the world's population who are children are excluded. This clear, straightforward message can be used to challenge economists and political and social scientists to begin to address the issues. They should be asked to consider seriously the effect of the exclusion of children, as well as the eventual inclusion of children, on their descriptions, analyses and understandings of social realities and their prescriptions for economic, political and social actions.

Similarly, studies – both quantitative and qualitative – of the social and economic costs to society, now and in the future, of the lack of recognition of the 'citizen child' are urgently needed. The information such studies could furnish is vital for the deepening of awareness and the generation of political commitment.

For practical purposes we can distinguish two major levels at which first steps need to be taken and can be taken. One is the level of the person or persons who care. This level is always a 'local' one and extends from parents to members of the immediate neighbourhood or locality. At this level, chapters of non-government organizations, teachers, motivated parents and others could help establish local groups within, for instance, a parent-teacher organization. Such groups could collect highly accurate information related to children and form action committees to achieve priorities which have been identified locally. They could also fill other needs. Thus, they could discuss the Convention on the Rights of the Child, inform others about the implications of the Convention and, most importantly, explore social and economic processes affecting children and monitor the overall progress – or lack of progress – at the local level. The reliance mainly on national level institutions for monitoring is neither a sufficient nor a practical way to turn child rights, partly or wholly, into reality. There must be decisive initiatives and effective monitoring in the places where the children live and where the problems exist. Another priority at the local level is the formation of appropriate children's groups. These groups could become instruments for meaningful interaction between children and involved adults. Exchanges on the different ways in which children and adults map and evaluate the characteristics and problems of the lives of children could be very educational and rewarding.

The second context in which action needs to be initiated immediately is the political level. This level covers communes, counties or corresponding units, district or regional structures and central authorities and the national government. National non-government organizations working for and with children and other advocates for children need to establish routine interactions focused on local or national priorities and on the findings emanating from monitoring and other initiatives carried out locally. New information on children and childhood requested from and supplied by the research community should be fed into this ongoing dialogue. The creation of opportunities for the involvement of children in the dialogue should be a priority for immediate action at this level.

If action along these lines could be undertaken in some places (or documented in cases in which it is already under way), we could begin to change the climate and move towards a more realistic recognition of children, their talents and their contributions, as well as towards the creation of better opportunities for children and towards the more effective allocation and application of the resources which rightfully belong to children as citizens.

On the global level, mobilization for child-centred development and children's rights needs strengthening. This will require enlightened and energetic leadership, and innovative forms of international cooperation. Compared with a long postwar period when the scene was dominated by UNICEF and a few internationally active NGOs, the present situation is radically different. The number of NGOs on all continents engaged, not only nationally but also internationally, has increased dramatically. Many organizations such as WHO, UNDP, other UN agencies and the World Bank are either directly or indirectly involved in development related to children. The advent of the Convention on the Rights of the Child has further expanded international activities. The efforts to reform the work of the United Nations may lead to new approaches demanding further integration of work.

In spite of these changes, the mechanisms for sharing information and for the division of labour according to principles of comparative advantages among various partners are today weak in the field of development for children. Fragmentation of efforts and a certain isolation in approaches still dominate. To some extent this can be explained by the need of many organizations to foster images and profiles that can facilitate fundraising. Other reasons are to be found in institutional history, existing organizational cultures and long-standing differences between intergovernmental agencies and NGOs. There are good reasons to believe that multiplicity and a certain competitiveness – where different actors focus on what they are good at – constitute a healthy climate for development. In spite of this, however, there is today a strong need for a global forum in which major partners could participate on equal terms for information sharing, consensus building and creating respect for diversity, sharing in tasks, sharpening advocacy and mobilizing commitment. An important purpose would be to learn to know each other's organizations and work, to organize urgent research on aspects of betterment for children, to initiate assessment and evaluation of experiences and to identify the best available knowledge and practices.

A forum of this character – an International Children's Council – could help to dispel public dissatisfaction with unnecessary and destructive manifestations of competitiveness and existing misunderstandings that negatively affect development for children. In order to be practical and useful, efforts in this direction should be gradual. They could start with informal groupings of the leaders of international agencies and internationally working NGOs from all continents. It would be important to have representatives of children and young people involved. To be meaningful one or two annual contacts would be required apart from more frequent interaction when the cooperation has been started. Similarly one or two topics should be selected for in-depth consideration in a phased process to evolve a working mechanism responding to real, rather than to perceived, needs.

A major task of a new and cooperative mechanism for child-centred development would be to assist in the global implementation of children's rights. Although the implementation of the Convention on the Rights of the Child will be slow – most probably a never-ending process – there are some dramatic violations of children's rights in local communities, in the nations to which these belong and also internationally that require massive attention. My comments are limited to a few situations where breaches of human rights and the consequent denial of citizenship are especially serious and unconscionable. The argument is not that some rights are 'more right' than others. The argument is that some violations of rights need to be more urgently addressed and dealt with. This will require new approaches by the international community, its agencies and institutions. The issues deserving special and immediate international (and national) attention are:

1. circumstances of bonded child labour: figures circulating are in the tens of millions;
2. circumstances of commercial sexual exploitation of children: recent estimates of around 2 million involved and of many millions of violations taking place every week were made at the World Congress against Commercial Sexual Exploitation of Children in Stockholm in 1996;
3. circumstances of exposure of children to war and other forms of organized or large-scale violence: many millions of children have been so exposed during the last decade.

In the three selected circumstances the opportunities for effective prevention and protection on the local level are weak or non-existent. The protective ambitions in the child's immediate environment are either eroded or powerless. The balance of power is severely tilted in favour of those who abuse, exploit and put children at risk.

On the national level there often exist legal provisions against bonded labour, sexual exploitation or exposure to the hazards of war, but these provisions are just as often not enforced. On the contrary, sometimes those in charge of, and accountable for, the protection have been found to actively sabotage the child's rights and collude with the perpetrators of the abuse. The victimized children and their carers have neither the knowledge, the social positions or the means to utilize existing legal channels. There must therefore be effective mechanisms to seek, find and eradicate violations. For this to happen there must be strong advocacy and a fundamental change of mindsets among the public and politicians alike in support of decisive political action. These conditions either do not exist or are too weak in all the three circumstances mentioned here, although many social activists and NGOs are trying hard to expose the problems and to create a new and favourable social climate for action. Strong international support is needed.

So far international responses, by intergovernmental and non-governmental organizations alike, to the sexual exploitation of children, abuse of bonded labour and children in war have mainly taken the form of advocacy, building on available information and the international consensus on children's rights. Another response has been in the form of efforts to contain and limit problems by international campaigns such as End Child Prostitution in Asian Tourism (ECPAT) and the recent Congress against Commercial Sexual Exploitation of Children sponsored by the Swedish Government, ECPAT, the NGO Group for the Convention on the Rights of the Child and UNICEF. In the case of bonded labour and child labour in general, similar international campaigns have been launched by alliances of NGOs, governments and the private sector to expose and limit the market for goods produced with the involvement of child labour. In the case of children in war, the Red Cross and Red Crescent together with organizations like Médecins sans Frontiers and others have continued their policy of protective activities in crisis situations. Initiatives to create days of tranquillity in war situations in Africa and Latin America were taken in the mid-1980s by UNICEF to provide opportunities for regular preventive health care for children. The concept of corridors of peace for the provision of food to children and other civilians in war has also been tried. A number of studies of children exposed to war either as victims or as child soldiers have been done, culminating in the recently published report to the General Assembly by Graça Machel.

All these efforts have contributed to creating a new global awareness and search for protective and remedial action which can be facilitated or promoted by the international community and its intergovernmental and non-governmental organizations. However, in comparison with other areas of child rights such as the right to survival, the right to health and the right to education, efforts in joint international action in the three problem areas discussed here have been feeble. Not only are these situations complicated and infected by the existence of vested interests and protection in high places. Global organizations and institutions have also been unable to take an active role in these matters as they lack the power of enforcement and the necessary political and legal authority. These restrictions have to be dealt with as a matter of urgency. Disregarding for the moment the massive advocacy and programmatic work done by a great number of international and national NGOs and by UNICEF, ILO and others, this urgency is illustrated by the fact that there exists today only an international advisory body to oversee the vast field of children's rights, including the ongoing violations that are discussed here. It is the Committee on the Rights of the Child. It is comprised of 10 members who are elected in their individual capacity. It has an impressive monitoring and advisory mandate which generates an enormous workload. In spite of this it is seriously understaffed and underfunded. The dearth and weaknesses of institutional mechanisms starkly expose the inability of the international community to shoulder a collective responsibility for protection against some of the most heinous violations of children's rights where the national and local levels are either disinterested or unable to offer protection.

It is therefore time to propose new initiatives. Using the accepted global standards laid down in the Convention of the Rights of the Child, ways must be found to define bonded child labour, commercial sexual exploitation of minors and the unprotected exposure of children to modern warfare as 'Crimes Against Humanity'. These violations should be moved to the same level and regarded with the same seriousness as other crimes against humanity. They deserve the same international and national responses. Similarly, negligence in providing proper protection for the victims of these crimes should be declared to be a crime of complicity. Not only are the violations of children's rights in these instances morally revolting and ethically unacceptable. It is similarly unconscionable that the international community has found it possible to create supranational rules and institutions to deal with crimes of war and to some extent with international terrorism but not with the planned and unscrupulous destruction of the minds and bodies, and future lives of its children. The proposal is not to abandon advocacy, mobilization, research, political work, international networking, or any existing or future programmes to better the situation of children. Those should be progressed in an incremental way. But in areas of outright criminal behaviour of adults against minors, an incremental, developmental approach is not enough. It must be complemented by international criminalization of those violations that from an ethical and legal perspective constitute indisputable crimes. Nobody would argue for an incremental, developmental approach for dealing with murder nationally or internationally. It is equally absurd to recommend such an approach for the crimes of bonded labour, commercial sexual exploitation of children or their unprotected exposure to warfare.

The solutions will not be easy to find. But they must be found. We cannot enter into this debate here and now, but we can note that it will be necessary to revise relevant international instruments on the definition of crimes against humanity, and to set up internationally and nationally recognized and supported 'search and action' teams, and vastly increased research, information, publicity and advocacy efforts. The process of broadening to the international level responsibility and accountability for dealing with some of the ongoing massive crimes against the citizen child must begin in earnest. Although international legal action is extremely delicate and difficult, the very fact that the label 'Crime against Humanity' can be applied will in itself provide a powerful tool. However, we need to be prepared, as many before us in similar situations, to be met with the well-known comment that what we are suggesting is impossible. The only answer, which also has famous precedents, is that it is necessary.

Long-term challenges

Betterment for children is part of the moral history of mankind. Regardless of place or time, this history is about the liberation of the oppressed and the inclusion of the excluded. It is based on the assumption that all members of mankind possess an inherent and equal 'human' value. It is a history with a purpose: the establishment of equity in the opportunities to lead a life in which suffering is reduced and well-being and meaning are augmented, a life in which all – including the marginalized – can realize their physical, mental and spiritual potentials and achieve greater control of their individual and collective destinies.

The immediate neighbours in the recent history of the effort to improve the situation of children are the processes of decolonization and national liberation that began with the American Revolution and have flowed during the last 200 years across Europe, Latin America, Asia and Africa.

The struggle of oppressed classes which was stimulated by the French Revolution spread into the struggle against slavery and continues today through movements for democracy, civil and human rights and the women's movement. Attempts to achieve recognition for the value, dignity and identity of neglected or suppressed groups with common ethnicity and shared lifestyles and views are being given a strong voice in an increasingly interdependent world.

It is within this background that the vision of the global movement for children and the betterment of their condition belongs. To realize this vision, knowledge and practice must be joined together in order to create a social, cultural and ethical climate in which the needs and rights of children no longer have to be constantly argued and negotiated but are regarded as normal and valued goals for society and its members.

The time has come to seize every opportunity to highlight the issue of children, their rights and the condition of their childhood by combining the compassion of the private concern with the responsibility and the resources in the public domain.

The time has come for the research community to devote interest and energy to the problems facing children in a period of changing lives and accelerating social and cultural transformations. Why should there be Nobel Prizes for those who have understood nature's physical properties, but not for significant advances in the knowledge of the nature and conditions of Man's 'reality room' and of issues related to the quality and betterment of life? Why should these be less important than the exploration of the behaviour of the cosmos or the dance of sub-atomic particles? The appalling absence of data in both rich and poor countries relevant to children and from the perspectives of the lives of children – apart from some crude statistics – is in itself a severe indictment of the neglect and lack of responsibility of governments and of the scientific community.

The time has come for politicians who seek public office to understand that they must not only be faithful to the constitution of their respective countries, but also to the Convention on the Rights of the Child and to the solemn commitments embodied in the National Programmes of Action for Children adopted by the World Summit for Children, including the reallocation of resources – intellectual, human and financial – that these entail.

The time has come to take our intergenerational obligations seriously and to discuss the structure of the international system which needs to evolve for the next century and especially to analyse and articulate the policies, the institutions and the resources which will be required by those of our citizens who are going to inhabit the next century.

All over the world ideologies are crumbling. This does not alter the fact that the world possesses a tremendous resource of moral and intellectual energy in its children and in all the young people who are in search of meaning and purpose. We have a rare opportunity – an historic opportunity – if only we can capture this energy and articulate a new vision of a global community with the child in the midst, surrounded by a supportive environment, physical and social, and the peace and emotional security which children need to develop into creative and confident human beings. This is a trinity which, whatever our worldviews and our convictions, we can recognize as a symbol of deep meaning and purpose for everyone on this earth.

If we can give words to these possibilities and translate them into meaningful action, we might be able to begin to build a new solidarity among all people. In this, our children might be our strongest ally and our best hope. Indeed, solidarity with the child offers the opportunity to overcome the ugliness of the ethnicity or religiosity which are again threatening to divide the world into the 'us' and the 'them', a 'them' whom the 'us' refuse to care for and sometimes feel free to destroy. Solidarity with the child is one of the few bridges left that still has the strength to connect the North and the South and to help us prevent the divisions of inequality and injustice within and among societies and nations that threaten to divide our world into separate planets.

The child needs us, but we need to adopt the perspective of the child if we are serious about improving lifestyles, realizing human betterment and managing the governance and security of a complex world. If we realize this, then perhaps this world can unite, step by step, not against something, but for something: a popular, professional and political movement – and a children's movement – for the child, with the child and around the child and the society which she is both part of and migrating towards, a movement which future historians will look upon as a major advance in the moral history of mankind. Ultimately, it might then be the powerless child who will provide the vision and the energy to make this earth a safer and a more wholesome planet for life in all its forms. That prospect is surely sufficient for recognizing at long last the citizen child.

Notes and references

1. See Edwards (1966).
2. Anand and Sen (1994). See also Chen and Singh (1995), page 13.
3. Chen and Singh (1995), page 13.
4. Among the recent pioneers have been Gunnar Myrdal, Hans Singer, Immanuel Wallerstein, Samir Amin, Andre Gunder Frank, Henrique Cardoso, Peter Worsley and Eric Wolf. Excellent and critical analyses of the extensive debate have been presented by Blomström and Hettne (1984), Friberg and Hettne (1985) and Daly and Cobb (1989). For a brief overview of the debate, see Knutsson (1996).
5. Kuhn (1962).
6. O'Dea (1993).
7. O'Dea (1993), page 9.
8. See Taylor *et al* (1995).
9. Bronfenbrunner (1990).
10. 'Dalit' is a low-caste or non-caste person. 'Harijan' means 'children of God', a euphemism coined by Mahatma Gandhi for people outside the Indian caste system. The quotation is taken from Arole (1995), page 39.
11. Arole (1995), page 41.
12. Arole (1995), page 41.
13. Arole (1995), page 41.
14. Arole (1995), page 42.
15. Arole (1995), page 49.
16. Arole (1995), page 50.
17. Based on personal discussions with the staff of the Bangladesh Rural Advancement Committee.
18. This discussion on knowledge for betterment owes much to Thomas Matthai, former senior policy adviser for the UNICEF Regional Office for South Asia, and to staff papers prepared by him.

19. The Convention on the Rights of the Child: Articles 2, 7–8, 23, 26 and 40.
20. The Convention on the Rights of the Child: Articles 6 and 24.
21. The Convention on the Rights of the Child: Articles 3, 9, 11, 16, 19–22, 24–5, 30, 32–8 and 40.
22. The Convention on the Rights of the Child: Articles 18, 23–4, 26, 31 and 39.
23. The Convention on the Rights of the Child: Articles 4, 12–15, 17–18, 23–4, 26–7, 29–31 and 39–40.
24. For example, see Alston, Parker and Seymour (1992). On these issues there is already an enormous amount of printed material. Useful overviews have been published by UNICEF and the UNICEF International Child Development Centre in Florence, Save the Children–UK and especially by members of the UN Committee on the Rights of the Child.
25. Parker (1994), Himes (1995) and De Vylder (1996).

Bibliography

Alanen, L. (1994), 'Gender and Generation: Feminism and the "Child Question"', in J. Qvortrup, M. Bardy, G. Sgritta and H. Wintersberger (eds) (1994), *Childhood Matters: Social Theory, Practice and Politics*, Aldershot, UK: Avebury.

Aldo, L. (1982), *A Sand County Almanac*, New York: Ballantine Books.

Alston, P. (ed.) (1994), *The Best Interests of the Child: Reconciling Culture and Human Rights*, Oxford: Clarendon Press.

Alston, P., S. Parker and J. Seymour (eds) (1992), *Children, Rights and the Law*, Oxford: Clarendon Press.

Anand, S. and A. Sen (1994), 'Sustainable Human Development: Concepts and Priorities', *Working Papers*, Cambridge, MA: Centre for Population and Development Studies, Harvard University.

Apthorpe, R. (ed.) (1986), *Development Studies: Critique and Renewal*, Leiden, The Netherlands: E.J. Brill.

Ariès, P. (1962), *Centuries of Childhood*, London: Jonathan Cape.

Arizpe, L. (ed.) (1996), *The Cultural Dimension of Global Change*, Paris: UNESCO.

Arnstein, S.R. (1979), 'Eight Rungs on the Ladder of Citizen Participation', *Journal of the American Institute of Planners*, July.

Arole, M. (1995), 'Jamkhed', in C. Taylor, A. Desai, K.E. Knutsson, P. O'Dea-Knutsson and D. Taylor-Ide (eds) (1995), *Partnerships for Social Development: A Casebook*, Baltimore: Future Generations, in cooperation with the Department of International Health, Johns Hopkins University.

Aseniero, G. (1985), 'Reflection on Developmentalism: From Development to Transformation', in UNU (1985), *Development as Social Transformation: Reflections on the Global Problematique*, Tokyo: United Nations University.

Bagehot, W. (1953), *Economic Studies*, Stanford, CA: Academic Reprints.

Banuri, T., G. Hydén, C. Juma and M. Rivera (1994), 'Sustainable Human Development, From Concept to Operation: A Guide for the Practitioner',

UNDP Discussion Papers, New York: United Nations Development Programme.

Bardy, M., J. Qvortrup, G. Sgritta and H. Wintersberger (eds) (1990), 'Childhood as a Social Phenomenon: A Series of National Reports', *Eurosocial Reports*, Vol. 36, Nos 1–17. Vienna: European Centre for Social Welfare Policy and Research.

Barth, F. (1987), *Cosmologies in the Making: A Generative Approach to Cultural Variation in Inner New Guinea*, Cambridge, UK: Cambridge University Press.

Baster, N. (ed.) (1972), *Measuring Development*, London: Frank Cass.

Black, M. (1986), *The Children and the Nations: The Story of UNICEF*, Oxford: Oxford University Press.

Blanchet, T. (1996), *Lost Innocence, Stolen Childhoods*, Dhaka, Bangladesh: University Press Limited.

Blankenhorn, D., D. Bayme and J.B. Elshtain (eds) (1990), *Rebuilding the Nest: A New Commitment to the American Family*, Milwaukee, WI: Family Service America.

Blomström, M. and B. Hettne (1984), *Development Theory in Transition*, London: Zed Books.

Bohm, D. and F.D. Peat (1987), *Science, Order and Creativity*, London: Bantam Books.

Both, D. (ed.) (1994), *Rethinking Social Development: Theory, Research and Practice*, London: Longman.

Boulding, E. (1979), *Children's Rights and the Wheel of Life*, New Brunswick, NJ: Transaction Books.

Boulding, K.E. (1978), *Ecodynamics: A New Theory of Societal Evolution*, London: Sage Publications.

Boulding, K.E. (1985a), *Human Betterment*, London: Sage Publications.

Boulding, K.E. (1985b), *The World as a Total System*, London: Sage Publications.

Bourdieu, P. (1977), *Outline of a Theory of Practice*, Cambridge, UK: Cambridge University Press.

Bourdieu, P. (1990), *In Other Words: Essays toward a Reflective Sociology*, Oxford: Polity.

Brokensha, D.W., D.M. Warren and O. Werner (eds) (1980), *Indigenous Knowledge Systems and Development*, Lanham, MD: University Press of America.

Bronfenbrenner, U. (1979), *The Ecology of Human Development: Experiments by Nature and Design*, Cambridge, MA: Harvard University Press.

Bronfenbrenner, U. (1990), 'Discovering What Families Do', in D. Blankenhorn, D. Bayme and J.B. Elshtain (eds) (1990), *Rebuilding the Nest: A New Commitment to the American Family*, Milwaukee, WI: Family Service America.

Bruce, J., C.B. Lloyd and A. Leonard, with P.L. Engle and N. Duffy (1995),

Families in Focus: New Perspectives on Mothers, Fathers and Children, New York: Population Council.

Burman, E. (1994), *Deconstructing Developmental Psychology*, London: Routledge.

Caldwell, B.M. (1983), 'Child Development and Cultural Diversity', *Future*, Vol. 8.

Chambers, R. (1983), *Rural Development: Putting the Last First*, London: Longman.

Chambers, R. (1993), *Challenging the Professions*, London: Intermediate Technology Publications.

Chen, L.C. and S. Singh (1995), 'Sustainability of the Children's Summit Goals: Concepts and Strategies', *Working Papers*, Cambridge, MA: Centre for Population and Development Studies, Harvard University. Mimeo.

Corbridge, S. (1994), 'Post-Marxism and Post-Colonialism: The Needs and Rights of Distant Strangers', in D. Both (ed.) (1994), *Rethinking Social Development: Theory, Research and Practice*, London: Longman.

Cornia, G.A., R. Jolly and F. Stewart (eds) (1987), *Adjustment with a Human Face*, Vol. 1: *Protecting the Vulnerable and Promoting Growth*, New York: Oxford University Press.

Corsini, C.A. and M. Grieco (1991), *Historical Perspectives on Breastfeeding*, Florence: Istituto degli Innocenti and UNICEF International Child Development Centre.

Corsini, C.A. and P.P. Viazzo (1993), *The Decline of Infant Mortality in Europe*, Florence: Istituto degli Innocenti and UNICEF International Child Development Centre.

Council of Europe (1995), 'Report on a European Strategy for Children by the Social, Health and Family Affairs Committee, Rapporteur Mr Cox, United Kingdom, 14 December 1995', Council of Europe. Mimeo.

Cunningham, H. (1991), *The Children of the Poor: Representations of Childhood since the Seventeenth Century*, Oxford: Blackwell.

Cunningham, H. (1995), *Children and Childhood in Western Society since 1500*, London: Longman.

Dahl, G. (1993), 'The Concept of Culture', Stockholm: Department of Social Anthropology, Stockholm University. Mimeo.

Dahl, G. and A. Hjort (1984), 'Development as Message and Meaning', *Ethnos*, Vol. 12, No. 3–4.

Daly, H.E. and J.B. Cobb Jr. (1989), *For the Common Good: Redirecting the Economy toward Community, the Environment and a Sustainable Future*, Boston: Beacon Press.

Dasgupta. P. (1993), *An Inquiry into Well-being and Destitution*, London: Oxford University Press.

de Mause, Lloyd (ed.) (1976), *The History of Childhood*, London: Souvenir Press.

de Sismondi, J.C.L. Simonde (1827), *Nouveaux Principes d'Economie Politique ou de la Richesse dans ses Rapports avec la Population*, Paris.

De Vylder, S. (1995), 'Sustainable Human Development and Macro-economics', *UNDP Discussion Papers*, New York: United Nations Development Programme.

De Vylder, S. (1996), 'Children's Rights, Development Strategies and Macroeconomic Policies', *Discussion Papers*, Stockholm: Rädda Barnen. Mimeo.

De Winter, M. (1995), 'Children, Fellow Citizens: Participation by Children and Young People as a Social Perspective of Education', *BSA Texts*.

Edwards, M. (1994), 'New Directions in Social Development Research: The Search for Relevance', in D. Both (ed.) (1994), *Rethinking Social Development: Theory, Research and Practice*, London: Longman.

Edwards, M. (1995), 'The Getting of Wisdom: Educating the Reflective Practitioner', in N. Hamdi (ed.) (1995), *Education for the Rest*, London: Intermediate Technology Publications.

Edwards, M. (1996), 'New Approaches to Children and Development: Introduction and Overview', in M. Edwards (ed.) (1996), 'Policy Arena: The Last Frontier?: Making Children Count in Development Policy and Practice', *Journal of International Development*, September.

Esteva, G. (1992), 'Development', in W. Sachs (ed.) (1992), *The Development Dictionary: A Guide to Knowledge as Power*, London: Zed Books.

Etzioni, A. (1988), *The Moral Dimension: Toward a New Economics*, New York: The Free Press.

Feyerabend, P. (1975), *Against Method: Outline of an Anarchistic Theory of Knowledge*, London: Verso.

Feyerabend, P. (1978), *Philosophy in a Free Society*, London: Verso.

Forss, K., B. Cracknell and N. Stromquist (1997), 'Learning in Development Cooperation: An Essay'. Draft, mimeo Ministry of Foreign Affairs, Stockholm.

Foucault, M. (1977), *Discipline and Punish*, London: Allen Lane.

Freeman, M.D.A. (1992), 'Taking Children's Rights more Seriously', in P. Alston, S. Parker and J. Seymour (eds) (1992), *Children, Rights and the Law*, Oxford: Clarendon Press.

Friberg, M. and B. Hettne (1985), 'The Greening of the World: Toward a Non-deterministic Model of Global Processes', in UNU (1985), *Development as Social Transformation: Reflections on the Global Problematique*, Tokyo: United Nations University.

Geertz, C. (1959), 'Ritual and Social Change: A Javanese Example', *American Anthropologist*, No. 61.

Geertz, C. (1973), *The Interpretation of Cultures*, New York: Basic Books.

Geertz, C. (1983), *Local Knowledge: Further Essays on Interpretive Anthropology*, New York: Basic Books.

Glazer, N. and D.P. Moynihan (1975), *Ethnicity, Theory and Experience*, Cambridge, MA: Harvard University Press.

Grubb, N.W. and M. Lazerson (1982), *Broken Promises*, New York: Basic Books.

Gurr, T. (1993), *Minorities at Risk: A Global View of Ethnopolitical Conflict*, Washington, DC: United States Institute of Peace.

Hamdi, N. (ed.) (1995), *Education for the Rest*, London: Intermediate Technology Publications.

Hart, R. (1992), 'Children's Participation: From Tokenism to Citizenship', *Innocenti Essays*, No. 4 Florence: UNICEF International Child Development Centre.

Hechter, M. (1987), *Principles of Group Solidarity*, Berkeley, CA: University of California Press.

Helleiner, G., G.A. Cornia and R. Jolly (1991), 'IMF Adjustment Policies and Approaches and the Needs of Children', *World Development Library*, Oxford: Pergamon Press.

Hewlett, S.A. (1993), *Child Neglect in Rich Nations*, New York: UNICEF.

Himes, J.R. (ed.) (1995), *Implementing the Convention on the Rights of the Child: Resource Mobilization in Low-income Countries*, The Hague: Martinus Nijhoff.

Hobart, M. (1993), *An Anthropological Critique of Development: The Growth of Ignorance*, London: Routledge.

Horowitz, D. (1985), *Ethnic Groups in Conflict*, Berkeley, CA: University of California Press.

IDRC (1995), 'Spirituality, Culture and Economic Development', *IDRC Working Papers*, 22 November. Ottawa: International Development Research Centre.

James, A. and A. Prout (eds) (1990), *Constructing and Reconstructing Childhood: Contemporary Issues in the Sociological Study of Childhood*, London: Palme Press.

Jenks, C. (1996), *Childhood*, London: Routledge.

Jolly, R. (1993), 'Human Development: Elements and Questions for a Paradigm of Action', New York: UNICEF. Mimeo.

Jonsson, U. (1996), 'Human Rights and Human Development Goals', Kathmandu: UNICEF Regional Office for South Asia. Mimeo.

Kent, G. (1995), *Children in the Political Economy*, London: Macmillan.

Kessel, F.S. and A.W. Siegel (eds) (1983), *The Child and Other Cultural Inventions*, New York: Praeger.

Key, Ellen (1900), *Barnens ärhundrade (The Century of the Child)*, Stockholm: Bonniers. (In Swedish)

Knutsson, K.E. (1970), 'Fieldnotes from Work among the Oromo of Ethiopia', Manuscript.

Knutsson, K.E. (1979), 'The Concept of Development: A Logical Invalid', *Research and Progress*, Stockholm: Royal Academy of Science.

Knutsson, K.E. (1980), 'Culture Research – Tool or Decoration: Reflections on the Role of Humanities', *Yearbook of the Royal Academy of History and Literature*. (In Swedish)

Knutsson, K.E. (1985), 'Immunizing for Development', *Carnet des Enfants*, Vol. 69/72.

Knutsson, K.E. (1986), *Universities and the Production of Knowledge*, Oslo: Oslo University Press.

Knutsson, K.E. (1991), 'Social Deficiencies, Biological Rebellions: Presidential Address'. Paper presented at the 'Commonwealth Conference on Diarrhoea and Malnutrition', New Delhi. Mimeo.

Knutsson, K.E. (1994), 'Social and Cultural Aspects of International Child Health: International Child Health, Achievements and Future Challenges', *News on Health Care in Developing Countries*, Vol. 7 Uppsala, Sweden.

Knutsson, K.E. (1996), 'Social Fields and Cultural Constellations: Reflections on Some Aspects of Globalization', in L. Arizpe (ed.) (1996), *The Cultural Dimension of Global Change*, Paris: UNESCO.

Korten, D.C. and F.B. Alfonso (eds) (1983), *Bureaucracy and the Poor: Closing the Gap*, West Hartford, CT: Kumarian Press.

Korten, F.F. and R. Siy Jr. (1989), *Transforming a Bureaucracy: The Experience of the Philippine National Irrigation Administration*, West Hartford, CT: Kumarian Press.

Kuhn, T. (1962), *The Structure of Scientific Revolutions*, Chicago: University of Chicago Press.

Lansdown, G. (1995), *Taking Part: Children's Participation in Decisionmaking*, London: Institute for Public Policy Research.

Levine, J. (1994), *Getting Men Involved: Strategies for Early Childhood Programmes*, New York: Scholastic.

Liljeström, R. (1983), 'The Public Child, the Commercial Child and Our Child', in F.S. Kessel and A.W. Siegel (eds) (1983), *The Child and Other Cultural Inventions*, New York: Praeger.

Matthai, T. (ed.) (1992), 'South Asia Consultations on Achieving the Goals of the 1990s for Children and Development', Faridabad, India: Thomson Press.

Maxwell, N. (1984), *From Knowledge to Wisdom*, Oxford: Basil Blackwell.

Mead, M., and M. Wolfenstein (eds) (1955), *Childhood in Contemporary Cultures*, Chicago: University of Chicago Press.

Morgan, E. (1994), *The Descent of the Child: Human Evolution from a New Perspective*, London: Souvenir Press.

Moynihan, D.P. (1993), *Pandemonium*, Oxford: Oxford University Press.

Mutuku, M. and R. Mutiso (1994), 'Kenya: The Urban Threat to Women and Children', in C. Szanton Blanc (ed.) (1994), *Urban Children in Distress: Global Predicaments and Innovative Strategies*, Yverdon, Switzerland: Gordon and Breach.

Muzaffar, C. (ed.) (1991), *The Human Being: Perspectives from Different Spiritual Traditions*, Penang, Malaysia: Alirai.

Myers, R. (1992), *The Twelve Who Survive: Strengthening Programmes of Early Childhood Development in the Third World*, London: Routledge.

Myrdal, G. (1957), *Rich Lands and Poor: The Road to World Prosperity*, New York: Harper.

NCU (1988), *Report of the National Commission on Urbanization*, New Delhi: National Commission on Urbanization.

Nisbet, R.A. (1969), *Social Change and History*, London: Oxford University Press.

Oakley, A. (1993), 'Women and Children First and Last: Parallels and Differences between Children's and Women's Studies', in J. Qvortrup (ed.) (1993), 'Childhood as a Social Phenomenon: Lessons from an International Project', *Eurosocial Reports*, No. 47. Vienna: European Centre for Social Welfare Policy and Research.

O'Dea, P. (1993), *Gender Exploitation and Violence: The Market in Women, Girls and Sex in Nepal*, Kathmandu: UNICEF.

Olsen, Frances (1992), 'Children's Rights: Some Feminist Approaches to the United Nations Convention on the Rights of the Child', in P. Alston, S. Parker and J. Seymour (eds) (1992), *Children, Rights and the Law*, Oxford: Clarendon Press.

O'Neill, J. (1994), *The Missing Child in Liberal Theory*, Toronto: University of Toronto Press.

O'Neill, O. (1985), 'Rights, Obligations and Needs', *Logos*, No. 6.

O'Neill, O. (1988), 'Ethical Reasoning and Ideological Pluralism', *Ethics*, No. 98.

O'Neill, O. (1992), 'Children's Rights and Children's Lives', in P. Alston, S. Parker and J. Seymour (eds) (1992), *Children, Rights and the Law*, Oxford: Clarendon Press.

Ortner, S. (1984), 'Theory in Anthropology since the Sixties', *Comparative Studies in Society and History*, Vol. 26, No. 1.

OUP (1971), *The Compact Edition of the Oxford English Dictionary*, Vol. I: *A–O*, New York: Oxford University Press.

PAHO (1995), 'The Impact of the Expanded Programme of Immunization and the Polio Eradication Initiative on Health Systems in the Americas: Final Report of the Taylor Commission', Washington, DC: Pan American Health Organization.

Parker, D. (1994), 'Resources and Child Rights: An Economic Perspective', *Innocenti Occasional Papers*, Child Rights Series, No. 6 (February), Florence: UNICEF International Child Development Centre.

Pinchbeck, I. and M. Hewitt (1973), *Children in English Society*, London: Routledge and Kegan Paul.

Ploman, E. (ed.) (1986), *The Science and Practice of Complexity*, Tokyo: United Nations University.

Popper, K.R. and J. Eccles (1977), *The Self and its Brain: An Argument for Inter-actionism*, New York: Springer.

Prigogine, I. and I. Stengers (1984), *Order Out of Chaos: Man's New Dialogue with Nature*, New York: Bantam Books.

Purdy, L.M. (1992), *In their Best Interest?: The Case against Equal Rights for Children*, Ithaca, NY: Cornell University Press.

Pylkanen, P. (1989), *The Search for Meaning: The New Spirit in Science and Philosophy*, Wellingborough, UK: The Aquarian Press.

Qvortrup, J. (ed.) (1993), 'Childhood as a Social Phenomenon: Lessons from an International Project', *Eurosocial Reports*, No. 47, Vienna: European Centre for Social Welfare Policy and Research.

Qvortrup, J., M. Bardy, G. Sgritta and H. Wintersberger (eds) (1994), *Childhood Matters: Social Theory, Practice and Politics*, Aldershot, UK: Avebury.

Rädda Barnen (1995), *Making Reality of the Rights of the Child*, Stockholm: Rädda Barnen.

Richardson, J. (1995), 'Achieving Gender Equality in Families: The Role of Males', *Innocenti Global Seminar Reports*, No. 6, Florence: UNICEF International Child Development Centre.

Ryan, W.F. (1995), *Culture, Spirituality and Economic Development*, Ottawa: International Development Research Centre.

Sachs, W. (ed.) (1992), *The Development Dictionary: A Guide to Knowledge as Power*, London: Zed Books.

Said, E. (1979), *Orientalism*, New York: Vintage Books.

SCF-UK (1995), *Toward a Children's Agenda: New Challenges for Social Develop-ment*, London: Save the Children-UK. (Prepared by Bill Bell, Andrew Chetley, Mike Edwards, Neil MacDonald and Angela Penrose)

Schumacher, E.F. (1968), 'Buddhist Economics', *Resurgence*, Vol. 1, No. 11.

Seers, D. (1969), 'What are We Trying to Measure'. Paper presented at the 11th World Conference of the Society for International Development, New Delhi. Reprinted in N. Baster (ed.) (1972), *Measuring Development*, London: Frank Cass.

Sen, A. (1987), *On Ethics and Economics*, Oxford: Blackwell.

Sklair. L. (ed.) (1994), *Capitalism and Development*, London: Routledge and Kegan Paul.

Snow, C.P. (1959), *The Two Cultures and a Second Look: An Expanded Version of the Two Cultures and the Scientific Revolution*, Cambridge, UK: Cambridge University Press.

Stafseng, O. (1993), 'A Sociology of Childhood and Youth: The Need of Both?', in J. Qvortrup (ed.) (1993), 'Childhood as a Social Phenomenon: Lessons from an International Project', *Eurosocial Reports*, No. 47, Vienna: European Centre for Social Welfare Policy and Research.

Stavenhagen, R. (1990), *The Ethnic Question*, Tokyo: United Nations Univer-sity.

Stiefel, M. and M. Wolfe (1994), *A Voice for the Excluded: Popular Participation in Development, Utopia or Necessity*, London: Zed Books.

Szanton Blanc, C. (ed.) (1994), *Urban Children in Distress: Global Predicaments and Innovative Strategies*, Yverdon, Switzerland: Gordon and Breach.

Tawney, R.H. (1926), *Religion and the Rise of Capitalism*, London: Harmondsworth.

Taylor, C., A. Desai, K.E. Knutsson, P. O'Dea-Knutsson and D. Taylor-Ide (eds) (1995), *Partnerships for Social Development: A Casebook*, Baltimore: Future Generations, in cooperation with the Department of International Health, Johns Hopkins University.

Therborn, G. (1993), 'Children's Rights since the Constitution of Modern Childhood: A Comparative Study of Western Nations', in J. Qvortrup (ed.) (1993), 'Childhood as a Social Phenomenon: Lessons from an International Project', *Eurosocial Reports*, No. 47, Vienna: European Centre for Social Welfare Policy and Research.

Törnebohm, H. (1974), 'An Essay on Knowledge Formation', *Reports from the Department of Theory of Science*, Gothenburg, Sweden: Department of the Theory of Science, University of Gothenburg.

UNDP (1993), *Human Development Report 1993*, New York: Oxford University Press.

UNICEF (1987), *The State of the World's Children 1987*, New York: UNICEF.

UNICEF (1990), 'First Call for Children: World Declaration and Plan of Action from the World Summit for Children, Convention on the Rights of the Child', New York: UNICEF.

UNICEF (1994), 'Challenges before the World Summit for Social Development: Perspectives from UNICEF', New York: UNICEF. Mimeo.

UNICEF (1995a), 'UNICEF Statement to the Social Summit', New York: UNICEF.

UNICEF (1995b), *The State of the World's Children 1995*, New York: Oxford University Press.

UNICEF (1995c), 'Poverty, Children and Policy: Responses for a Brighter Future', *Economies in Transition Studies*, Regional Monitoring Report, No. 3. Florence: UNICEF International Child Development Centre.

UNU (1985), *Development as Social Transformation: Reflections on the Global Problematique*, Tokyo: United Nations University.

Uphoff, N. (1992), *Learning from Gal Oya: Possibilities for Participatory Development and Post-Newtonian Social Science*, Ithaca, NY: Cornell University Press.

Van Bueren, G. (1995), 'The International Law and the Rights of the Child', *International Studies in Human Rights*, Vol. 35, Dordrecht, The Netherlands: Martinus Nijhoff.

von Wright, G. (1986), *Vetenskapen och Furnuftet (Science and Reason)*, Stockholm: Bonniers. (In Swedish) von Wright, G. (1993), *Myten om Framsteget (The Myth of Progress)*, Stockholm: Bonniers. (In Swedish)

von Wright, G. (1994), *Att Forsta sin Samtid (Understanding the Present)*, Stockholm: Bonniers. (In Swedish)

Wagner, D. and H. Stevenson (eds) (1982), *Cultural Perspectives on Child Development*, San Francisco: W.H. Freeman.

Waldrop, M.M. (1993), *Complexity: The Emerging Science at the Edge of Order and Chaos*, London: Viking.

Wallerstein, I. (1974), *The Capitalist World Economy*, Cambridge, UK: Cambridge University Press.

Wallerstein, I. (1982), 'Economic Theories and Historical Disparities of Development', São Paulo: Fernand Braudel Centre for the Study of Economics, Historical Systems and Civilizations. Mimeo.

Wallerstein, I. (1994), 'Development Lodestar or Illusion?', in L. Sklair (ed.) (1994), *Capitalism and Development*, London: Routledge and Kegan Paul.

Wallman, S. (ed) (1977), *Perceptions of Development*, Cambridge, UK: Cambridge University Press.

Were, M. (1978), 'Creating Areas of Understanding: Report on a Public Health Project', Nairobi: UNICEF.

West, A. (1996), 'But What is It?: A Critique of Undefined Participation', London: Save the Children-UK. Mimeo.

Whitehead, A.N. (1925), *Science and the Modern World*, New York: Macmillan.

Whitehead, A.N. (1929), *Process and Reality*, New York: Harper.

Whiting, B. and J.W.M. Whiting (1975), *Children of Six Cultures: A Psychocultural Analysis*, Cambridge, MA: Harvard University Press.

Wolf, E. (1982), *Europe and the People without History*, Berkeley, CA: University of California Press.

World Bank (1993), *World Development Report 1993*, New York: Oxford University Press.

Worsley, P. (1984), *The Three Worlds: Culture and Development*, Chicago: University of Chicago Press.

Zelizer, V.A. (1985), *Pricing the Priceless Child: The Changing Social Value of Children*, New York: Basic Books.

Index